DESERT DONS

The Truth behind the Young Soldiers

Who Turned Iraq from Chaos to Cartel

BEAU LE JEUNE

A percentage of all proceeds will be donated to Charitable Organizations
assisting the families of U.S. soldiers.

ISBN: 1-4392-2453-6
ISBN-13: 9781439224533
LCCN: 2009900085

Dedication

To Colonel Rock, thank you, sir.

Table of Contents

Foreword

I'm not sure what the foreword of a book should look like, but if it consists of an outside opinion from that of LeJeune's, then this should do it. The men had two sayings about LeJeune. My favorite is the latter.

"LeJeune just may be the baddest motherfucker you'll ever meet." And...

"If you don't know who LeJeune is, you'd better fuckin' ask somebody."

The fact that I asked LeJeune not to write this book was of no concern to him. Actually, he really never took advice from anyone; to be honest, any orders or advice would certainly be ignored. "You'd get better results if you'd just ask nicely," he'd say to any ranking officer. He was probably the most stubborn son of a bitch I'd ever met. I really don't think that he cared for anyone or anything, especially in the military. He always spoke of loyalty as if it were the most important quality in any one man, but when it came to his own loyalty, no one knew where it lay. Money was nothing to him; he'd rather give it away than save it, yet he was always on a continuous mission to make more. Vices were his one constant. I never knew a man to enjoy sin so much. His love for everything forbidden consumed him and anyone in contact with him. Power was another thing. He was respected more than any officer on base, and yet daily he contradicted it by searching for ways to entice hatred from others.

Mental stability...anyone there knew he was a genius. He could do with words what Beethoven could do with a piano. Half the time I just thought he made up words, but it sounded convincing. He knew history and military, current events and politicians. He was smart, but that had nothing to do with how insane everyone thought he was. Sometimes he was the life of the party, and sometime he isolated himself for weeks. He would stand up for any woman he felt was being disrespected, even if one of the guys cursed in their presence, yet he treated all of them like a burden. His life was a chess game, as if he always needed the situation to be against him, all while he talked about flying under the radar. He was one big contradiction.

While these *are* my true opinions of LeJeune, the fact is that I would happily follow him into battle on a moment's notice. The *fact* is that he has a demanding presence in any crowd and is no doubt a force to be reckoned with. The *fact* is that he is as hardened as they come. The *fact* is that if you couldn't beat him, you joined him, and I have yet to hear of anyone who beat him. The *fact* is that he was a scar on the face of the United States military, but scars give character. The *hard fact* is that LeJeune was an extremely interesting person, a great friend, and a horrible human being.

Viva La Anarchy
- Mark

In war, truth is the first casualty.

– Aeschylus

Introduction

This cold weather of 2006 reminds me of a story I was warned never to tell. It will most likely lead to imprisonment and persecution from the American public. I have no fear of that because, like so many other soldiers, I live in imprisonment every day. We lie to our families to keep them safe from what happened overseas. The stories that make a hardened soldier are told with a drunken tongue, but the stories of a drunken soldier are hard to tell. I'm sorry, I was trying to find a philosophical way to say that, when we're drunk, we're more likely to tell horror stories, stories of battle, and the scars that it's left, but it is much harder to tell the stories of pleasure and laughter and lust. The stories that bonded the soldiers will never be told to our families, for they are filled with drugs, sex, and more importantly, a second family, a complete opposite from the one back home, a family that, much like a passive Manson family, was lost. We felt isolated and alone, and the Lord knows that what you do when you're alone makes you the real person that you are. If the Lord is right about that, then we weren't people at all, we were animals.

In no way am I implying that your loved ones were part of this chaos, but have no illusions about my experience. I was one of a few on the top of the infamous VLA organization, an organization that ran a black-market operation that stretched through six units in three different battalions on one base. As a Black Hawk unit, my journeys also allowed me to meet more soldiers from more bases. I was one of the most well-known people in the Sunni triangle, and through everyone I've ever encountered, I've only met one who was a by-the-book, no bullshit, follow-me-boys and let's get this done, type. Major, you know who you are. I'm not saying the major was the only good soldier out of the crew. I would have put any one of my men against him on any day. We would out shoot, stab, steal, rape, pillage, plunder, live, love, and out party any man there, and that's what we thought the war was about. By the end of my tour, that's what the war *was* about.

If you weren't drinking, you were smoking hashish. If you weren't smoking, you were doing X. If you weren't doing X, you were probably doing a combination of the first two. There was more sex going on there than the *Real World: New Orleans* edition. Sons became alcoholics, mothers became whores, and wives became concubines. It was, to most of us, the Garden of Eden. It was just a coincidence that the supposed real Garden of Eden was only a couple miles south.

This all came with a price. I paid for it more than most, less than some, but be assured everyone paid for it. Most everyone I've talked to has paid with either loss of loved ones, drug addictions, or mental instability. This stems from the memories of who we were and the added stress of maybe getting killed at any time. Maybe that's just me; I don't know, I'm not a doctor. I do know that the ones who have paid with their lives will not be included in this book. I will not dishonor them with the smut of this literature for two reasons. The first is that I only befriended one man who has lost his life through the craziness, but it wasn't until after returning home. The second reason is that their ultimate sacrifice will mute any charges against them when it comes to us, the people living their freedom. To these men and women I apologize.

I also would like to apologize to the family members of soldiers who I know have also paid dearly. I hope no divorces will come of this writing if they haven't come already. I will not mention any real names so that no one can be assured of any infidelity. Also, I don't need any heartbroken fucks showing up at my home, thinking I ruined their marriage. For that matter, speaking generally of deployed soldiers, I don't need two hundred thousand of them showing up at my front step. Now, to all those affected directly by this story, that means the ones who are included in it, replaced name or not, enjoy memory lane and maybe when you're too old to be ashamed of it, you can show your grandkids.

My testament before I start this book is that I will be called a liar by many. Throughout the investigation that will ensue, documents will be lost and eyewitness soldiers will rebut my claims due to mounting pressure. I cannot say if the story is true. I will not sign my own confession, but I can say there were enough people there that it will be honored as the truth, if not now, then surely during any investigation. I will have two collaborators helping me remember the smaller, more irrelevant but humorous points. Now, remember to take into consideration that we were shit faced practically twenty-four hours a day for the last eight months of our deployment. To the people who were there, if the stories begin to get out of timeline, or if I forget some of you who were there, I'm sorry and I tried my best.

If you realize that you are included in this book, be cautious of telling anyone until you have read it all; you may wish that none of this ever comes to light.

Chapter One

The Beginning

Ten months into my tour, I found myself shackled hands to feet, two armed guards loading me into a Black Hawk bound for Baghdad, where awaited my lawyer and the military judge. This certain flight was also boarding a nervous-looking, light-skinned black woman. She was small in size, and I could understand her fear in this huge iron helicopter. She also was without a weapon. Maybe she was a contract civilian, or perhaps someone of more importance; I didn't know. Restricted by my shackles from sitting upright, I leaned into my legs. I must have resembled someone scared of flight or sick before takeoff; whatever it was, she patted me on the back to comfort me. My escorts tried to steer her away, but I guess she figured they were shaking their heads just to say, "He'll be OK" As the blades started turning, just before the volume became too much to hear anything, she leaned in and said, "Don't worry, the flight is only about ten minutes."

I smiled, knowing that, as many times as I'd taken this trip, it had never taken less than thirty. Maybe she told a small lie to hopefully give a scared soldier comfort. She was sweet. As I looked to share a smile with one of my escorts, I saw a hidden smirk and a very subtle head shake. He was begging me not to do anything, but also saying that he wouldn't try to stop me either. So I slowly turned my eyes until they made contact with hers, then I jerked my hands as quickly toward her as I possibly could, until the weight of my legs stopped my shackled hands inches from her throat. She jumped back into her seat with a loss of breath, then she slowly leaned to my escort to ask him a question. I'm sure he couldn't hear; the engines were nearing liftoff and, unless you have a headset on, you can't hear shit. She leaned back into her seat and stared directly out the window. I caught her eye once more that trip and let a smile creep over my face; she acknowledged with a smile. That was my way of returning the small, comforting lie.

Escorts on either side of me is truly the story of my life. My mother still tells stories of this to embarrass me in front of girlfriends. The first time was before I could remember. She says I was escorted to her by an elderly man at a wedding ceremony. Apparently, I had gotten away from her and pulled an American flag down onto a group of people watching the ceremony from the back entrance. The second time I can remember fairly well, but it still helps for someone older to tell it. It seems I squished all of our neighbors' peppers with my hands, and then commenced to rub my eyes. When my older brother and cousin found me, I had to be escorted back to my mother with eyes that resembled plums. The third time was in high school. I was caught skipping more times than Ferris Bueller; therefore, every time I had to go to the pisser, two seniors would come up from the office and walk me to my destination and back. The last one in the States was at a place known as MEPS. MEPS is the in-processing office for soldiers when first entering the military. It's where soldiers take a physical, drug test, and all the other go'damn tests they need. The problem was that the night before, they put me and a rag-tag team of pre-soldiers in a hotel room in New Orleans. After a good night on the town, we all missed our appointment. Two days later, they brought me back, as you guessed it, with escorts.

Alright, enough bullshit. Let's get down to it. Fast-forward three years later, post basic training and whisky school (military school for medics). My first Army National Guard unit handed me off to another undermanned, New Orleans based unit that was set to deploy to Iraq. I couldn't stand anyone in this unit, and from what I could see, they didn't care for us much either. Of this new unit, about thirty percent were transferred from my old unit. We stuck together, and they were so confused they didn't know who was coming or going, and we weren't going to help them figure it out. We showed up when we wanted, left when we wanted, and since we weren't on the roll call for four months, they were none the wiser. In fact, the first time they noticed us was when they were activated for Iraq and they were forced to make sure they were at full strength. Once our men and theirs were around each other enough, we knew the shit was gonna go past words.

Now, being activated is not the last straw; once you're activated, you begin preparation. Classes from each of the sections were to be taught to everyone. The idea was that everyone should know how to use all the equipment and have some basic skills in each department. Well, we treated it like a burden, passing soldiers in medical skills that had no business working on others. I didn't know the first go'damn thing about that radio with the phone on it. Passed the class and still didn't know a damn thing. We weren't prepared, but rumor had it that the light colonel was looking for his full bird (a promotion), so chances were we'd be boots in the sand by the first of the next year, which didn't give us a lot of time.

A couple weeks later, we received our orders, the last straw, and I didn't know then whether to laugh or cry, but now I do. I should have wept like a baby, we were far from being war ready and it was steadily getting worse. A sergeant from our unit came to the medical section to inform me that I was "access." Access meaning that there were already enough medics to fill the unit's medical needs, and I wasn't needed for the deployment. I believe their decision to make me access rather than anyone else was based on the fact that I had the least time in the unit, it couldn't have been a rank issue being that I shared specialist rank with three out of four people in the medical section. Their plan was to leave me home for state side support or send me back to my old unit. The other two medics I had met through the activation could only wish to be in my shoes. I thought at that time that leaving then and there would have been a regretful decision, but actually opening the door of the captain's office would become my biggest regret.

As I entered his office, he looked up at me quickly and then back down at the tablet he was writing in.

"You were released. Why aren't you gone?"

"Sir, I don't think you understand..."

"Oh, let me guess, you want to get paid for this morning."

"No, sir, I'm coming with you."

"Now, don't you say that unless you mean it, because I'll make it happen."

"Well, make it happen, sir."

Yeah, as much as that sounds like bullshit to try to make myself look good, that's exactly how it happened. The best thing about it was that one of the witnesses was a helicopter refueler, and the other was a big mouth in headquarters. Word spread quickly, and people thought highly of me, which brings us to their first mistake.

Two days later, the captain found a place he could hide me within the ranks, and I began packing equipment with the rest of the unit. The medical equipment was too old to drag out, so we waited to get to Fort Polk to see what they had. The other medic and I became carpenters to build cargo boxes for the other sections to transfer their shit in. Three weeks of that and we were sitting in a convoy line ready to go to Fort Polk.

The night prior to the convoy was given to us to spend time with our families. It was of my own accord that mine didn't make a big deal over it. I hated pretty much anything to do with family, emotions, good-byes, and bullshit, maybe it was just the twenty year old rebelliousness, but now it's making me sad to think about it. I remember when all the families were hugging and kissing their loved ones, and finally the soldiers had to be pulled away to formation. When one of the soldiers asked about my family, all I could do was hit on one of the girls there.

"And who might that hot thing be?" I asked Mike, who was beside me.

Sgt. Defess snapped around. "That would be my fiancée."

"Huh, good taste," I said, trying to keep my eyes off her ass.

I always dealt with emotional shit like that, avoiding it like the plague. I don't know why, but sometimes I still do it to this day.

Chapter Two

Fort Polk: Home of the Mullet

Fort Polk. Our colonel explained it the best when he said there's no rearview mirror big enough to appreciate it. If that went over your head, it means that the best way to see it is through your rearview mirror, while you get as far away as you possibly can. It's Louisiana's largest training and mobilization station, surrounded by absolutely nothing. The city it resides in, Leeville, is economically based around soldiers spending money; hence, all the strip clubs. The women there were either married to soldiers, stripping, or driving a taxi. Now, as I think back on it, most of the strippers belonged in cages, so you can imagine the taxicab drivers were no prize, but that didn't stop my men. Actually, they weren't my men yet, but we'll move on. The girls there were the least of our problems. I hadn't been on active duty in three years and since then the National Guard has done nothing but make me soft and undisciplined. Being controlled again, especially by these idiots, was going to be my main issue.

As soon as we arrived, the Army badass bullshit started. The officers started being officers, and we, well, we started being us. They threw us into a set of barracks that had been condemned fifteen years before. Asbestos signs were posted all over. We laughed that off. They then implemented a salute policy. This policy stated that, in the barracks area, all enlisted must salute all officers. In theory, it should have worked. I mean, hell, it's been working like that for a couple hundred years now, but the collective voices of what were the beginnings of our crew derived a plan.

"Operation Dead Arm" commenced about a week after they decided to make the area a salute zone. We had the men salute as much as possible. While the laws of saluting decide where and when you can salute, we decided how to salute. In a group of soldiers only one must salute; therefore, the officer would return only one salute. Operation Dead Arm insisted that men walk at least five feet apart and never stand in groups, so the officer had to salute many times to our one each. If an officer decided not to be saluted for the rest of the day, all he would have to say is "I'll be here all day, men." Our men were to reply, "Sorry, sir, you've earned it," and snap a salute, thus forcing a return salute. We also had our special forces in ODA.

Wild Bill: 21, 6'4" - VLA Status: Special Forces. Morals: Medium. Wild Bill was one of the first members of the crew. A mulatto from the bayous of southern Louisiana, he had little respect for command and spoke frankly about any subject. He also belonged to POL, the helicopter refuelers, the largest group in our unit. He was very persuasive within his section.

Wild Bill was the only special operative in ODA. His mission was to coax the officers into saluting him in non-saluting areas. Being National Guard and not being accustomed yet to protocol, or maybe just the prospect of being recognized as the authority, officers rarely turned down a salute. We would then approach the officers, explain what they did wrong, make them feel like an ass, and leave. By the time they would turn to scold Wild Bill, he'd be gone. He once saluted from the inside of a school bus window and again hanging one-handed off the fire escape. He was an animal and more than welcome in our crew.

Two weeks after ODA began, the barracks area became a no-salute zone. It was one win for us in a line of many, but the command was far from defenseless. The next time they came, they would come with authority.

Training continued, equipment was issued, and meetings were held nightly to update the soldiers on information that would change in a day or two. Meetings were hot, cramped, and unproductive. Picture eighty men in your living room being lied to, not intentionally, but eventually they would become lies. We began to give the "wrap it up" signal, arm up, hand tilted in and pointing, moving in a circular motion. Through eighty people, it's hard to tell who's sending you the signal; maybe they would speed up this agonizing shit if they thought it was coming from a higher rank. Usually they would just apologize and say that they would try to get us out as fast as they could. To a civilian, this proves nothing;

to a soldier, this proves that the speaker, whatever rank they may be, is not an asshole. It would have been well within their right to make a scene.

"Do you have somewhere to be, soldier? Then put your arm down and listen!"

We began to rank the unit ourselves, through their actions: officers, members, neutrals, or enemies.

As we settled in and began to train in our own sections, the medical team was introduced to our flight doctor.

Col. Rock: 50 something, 5'8" - VLA Status: Inspiration. Morals: High. Col. Rock was a full-bird colonel with balls to match. To show his hierarchy, he used wisdom instead of authority. He was unsoldierly and hated the bureaucracy of the system. He never waited for things to happen; he did what was needed to complete the mission and was crucified for it at every turn. His actions inspired us to begin the VLA.

By the time we met Col. Rock, he had procured an office in the main hospital at Fort Polk. He had all the medics placed in the hospital with him to train. Though we weren't able to because of other preparations needed, it was a clear gesture of his personable skills. Not just anyone could waltz into a hospital, start his own practice, and request his personal staff work with him. Since we couldn't work together, he requested the medics drive him to the hospital and back to get to know us. He was a Republican Jew with daughters beautiful enough to end a war and a son he loved very much. I immediately took a liking to him and, I think, him to me.

It seemed to be a pretty easygoing section, but there was still one stepping stone. Sgt. LT. was the sergeant in charge of the medics.

Sgt. LT.: Mid 30s, 5'4" - VLA Status: Enemy. Morals: Low Medium. Sgt. LT. replaced a head medic whom everyone liked. A little young to be an E-7, we figured she screwed over a lot of soldiers to get where she was. Her favorite saying was "Do as I say and not as I do." The other females hated her for unknown reasons, something that would prove to be invaluable, later.

She was a tiny little black woman with the balls of a giant. If we had met on different terms, I would have enjoyed the way she dealt with the command, but she also dealt with us in an anal-retentive manner. We weren't on the same page, ever since I told her I thought she slept her way to the top and that she ran her section like a Mormon whorehouse. After that, she sent me an Article 15, which is a serious reprimand, and I drew a smiley face on it and filled in the comment section with, "Keep 'em coming." I had no respect for her or her authority. After that, no matter how hard she tried, and she did try, I couldn't bring myself to like her. Of course, Col. Rock stayed out of the affairs of the lower level unless it was detrimental. I needed something over her, and it wouldn't take long for her to hand it to me on a silver platter.

One weekend we were released without an off-post pass, which means we didn't have to report for the weekend, but we weren't allowed off base. After picking up some alcohol, we joined Sgt. LT. at her hotel room.

Breezy: 23 maybe, 5'11" - VLA Status: Member. Morals: Medium High. Breezy was a cop from New Orleans and part of the infamous intelligence section. His love for strippers and his quick wit made him one of my favorites. He was also the mastermind who tweaked the VLA operations to perfection.

Mic G: 26, 6'0" - VLA Status: Neutral. Morals: Medium. Mic G kept his distance from our organization in order to gain his brass (become an officer). His recognition was mostly through his roommate in Iraq, an officer in VLA. Although he had the characteristics of most of my men, he never claimed our organization.

We planned on a good night of drinking, some laughing, and then reporting back to the barracks. What unfolded was some drinking, some laughing, and some sweet, sweet lovemaking. Breezy and I left Mic G and Sgt. LT. at the hotel room to do what they do. Now, I'm not here to make assumptions, and just because they were lying in bed together doesn't give me the right to think anything else happened, but when we reported on Monday, Sgt. LT. called Mic G the "Beast Master." From that point forward, I figured I had something on her. The Uniformed Code of Military Justice, or UCMJ, clearly state that no soldiers can have sexual relations in their direct chain of command, unless they were together prior to their separations in rank. Just as a footnote, these two were married about a year and a half after our return from Iraq.

Married or not, it was my serious mistake to think I could use this over her. First, I would dance around that rule a few times myself, and second, no one gave a shit who was sleeping with whom out there. Everyone was either doing it themselves or trying to. I guess I was naive, but it didn't matter. I would never bring it up again until now.

As training went on, we started to become relaxed in our situation. The men would have a couple drinks each night, talk about the families they were leaving behind, and try to gain camaraderie. Soon, the couple of drinks every night became going out for drinks every night. On one of these nights, I finally got to sit down with a son-of-a-bitch who I thought was crazier than me.

AA: 26, 6'2" - VLA Status: Co Founder, Officer. Morals: None. AA apparently learned his skills through a fraternity. He was vile-humored, a mean drunk, and a sex addict. He managed to keep his sergeant rank through two counts of sexual harassment and a number of minor charges. Most VLA operations stemmed from his clever ideas, and his crew, DH3 and Big Vinnie.

DH3: 25, 5'7" - VLA Status: Member. Morals: Medium. DH3 was the friendliest member of the pack. Everyone loved DH3. He was respectful to officers and NCOs alike. He agreed with whatever AA said and would follow him to hell. He was very loyal, very motivated, but a weak drinker.

Big Vinnie: 22, 6'3" - VLA Status: Member; would become Officer. Morals: Low Medium. Vinnie made quite a statement wherever he went. He wasn't violent, but he looked it. He was an emotional Sicilian who would complain about anything to whoever would listen. During conversations, he would hip-hop dance and break into rap at a moment's notice; it didn't bother us much because most of his conversation was about his home town; Chalmette, a parish in Louisiana that most agree should be blown of the map.

Being from the motor pool, AA, DH3, and Big Vinnie were worked extremely hard, but they played to match. During a deep conversation about what I'm sure was the silicon-based economy of Eastern India, a plump young thing approached us with what I think was either her friend or a tumor protruding from her back. A couple drinks later and these three men would create one of the most told VLA stories.

Once the wolf pack (named after the motor pool's Sgt. Wulf) had gotten their beer goggles on straight, they rendezvoused at the girl's apartment. The gang then slept with the girl one after the other. AA, being the good leader he was, let his men go first. AA, being the sick bastard that he was, asked for her phone number and was rumored to tell someone he thought she really liked him. After all was done, she put on her dress and was out the door to meet her boyfriend.

Don't get me wrong, this was the most famous story, but it was only the second of three in the tizzle series. They were all with different girls and different groups, but all led by AA himself. The first was only with two, AA and another VLA officer.

Knight Ryder: 24, 5'10" - VLA Status: Officer. Morals: None. Knight Ryder was my medic counterpart. He could rebuild an engine or construct a house, your call. He would later become known as the "Virgin Destroyer." He was as cute as a button on panties, and if there ever was a button on panties, I'm sure he'd seen it...or had eaten it.

The third was with Breezy on a stripper they pulled out of Pegasus. They paid her eighty dollars apiece, and again AA came back to the barracks and claimed that she liked him. He thought a go'damn hooker fell in love with him. He was a mess.

These three events became known as the tizzle series. A rotizzle was AA and another, and the tritizzle was AA and two others. As the men came in at night, they would wake me up to let me know that they were up-to-date on their different tizzle certifications. Yes, the VLA began to certify the guys in our own skills. I began to think that AA had performance problems by himself, that he needed another set of nuts in the room to get him going. I don't regret to say that I was never certified in the tizzle qualifications myself, not that it stopped at Fort Polk and I didn't have enough time. In fact, it continued much into Iraq, and we even had VLA women certified, but there was no way I wanted to be behind closed doors with that sick, half-naked bastard. As a footnote, he once told me his first rotizle ever was when he was sleeping with a young mother and her infant son crawled out and started hugging on his leg.

"Technically there were two of us there." He stood his ground.

What a pervert.

The rifle range came and went, convoy training came and went, desert camouflage was issued, and our time in the States was getting short. Stress was coming down on everyone, and

AA decided to bring a couple of the guys for drinks at the local strip club. Little did AA know that one of the soldiers back at the barracks got drunk and took a swing at the first sergeant. The barracks were locked down, and everyone had to be accounted for. Since drinking wasn't allowed, nor was leaving base, AA was in a bind. The second lieutenant came to me for help; he knew I knew where they were and how to reach them, but when I called the strip club, they had just walked out with one of the strippers. AA and Breezy were about to drop off Giff, the third soldier, to put into effect the last stateside rotizzle, which I mentioned earlier.

Giff: 25, 5'8" - VLA Status: Officer. Morals: Low. Giff was Breezy's counterpart in the infamous intelligence section. His alcohol tolerance level didn't exist. He stayed shit-faced twenty-four hours a day but was always sensible. Giff would usually be the guy who told us to keep it down or remind us of our age.

Once Giff returned to the barracks and realized what was happening he contacted AA, and soon they would all be giving blood at the hospital for an alcohol test. Once the alcohol test came back positive, they all declared that they had taken NyQuil and that it contained enough alcohol to throw off the test. Once the results were in to the command, who were waiting at the hospital, they decided to do an alcohol sweep through the barracks. Punishment would come to anyone possessing alcohol, officers included. Luckily, Sgt. LT. was also at the hospital when this happened. She called Mic G and told him to hide the alcohol she had left in her locker. Mic G, trying to stay out of trouble, asked me to do it.

Now, when she reads this, I hope she doesn't put the blame on her husband for his bad judgment, but he handed her right to me. I made sure some of the other females, who despised her, witnessed me removing the liquor from her locker. I did as I was told and hid it, and then I ran upstairs to tell the guys that they were going to do a sweep. As I walked back to throw my own stash in the woods, I was almost hit by two or three dozen bottles being thrown from every direction, second-story windows and all. We made it through that one with the help of Sgt. LT. I thanked her, drank her Remy Martin, and had her in a corner. I was having a very good night. On the other hand, AA and the guys weren't as lucky. They were all reprimanded with Article 15s and began their punishments the next day. Extra duty, half pay, I can't remember, but I do know that it made AA want vengeance on every one of them sons of bitches. The command declared a victory, but they also turned AA into a bloodthirsty animal, which would, in turn, spawn the VLA.

That following week we were in the field practicing urban warfare. The sergeant major recruited a team of volunteers for the Downed Aircraft Recovery Team, DART for short.

Sgt. Maj.: mid 50s, 5'8" - VLA Status: Enemy. Morals: Medium. Sgt. Maj. would make a bad name for himself with the VLA by acquiring an off-post pass while at Fort Polk and sleeping at home every night, while the soldiers did not have that option. Also, Sgt. Maj. prided himself on being infantry, but he had spent all of his years without getting in the action. He wanted a fight so bad he was willing to risk a lot of men to get it.

These guys weren't the best soldiers, just the ballsiest. Of course, I volunteered as their flight medic to join in some of the festivities. During our high-speed training, I was summoned back to the medical tent to give shots. When I was finished, I decided to have a little fun with the DART crew. You see, they were the only ones to get night-vision goggles, and they were to patrol the outer perimeter of the foxholes the unit had built earlier. Well, I was issued NVGs also, so I recruited AA and we caused havoc for the rest of the night, taking potshots at them and moving to a different location. The two of us played cat and mouse with them for hours. It was sad to think that they were the elite of our unit. I didn't know whether to laugh or cry. Now I know I should have laughed; the boys were ready, and they'd prove themselves in Iraq.

Finally, orders came down; the flight was leaving that Monday, which gave us one night and the next whole day off. Since my hometown was too far away to visit and make it back on time, I called my longtime girlfriend to come up.

Hollie: 20, 5'9 - VLA Status: Civilian. Morals: High. Hollie and I began dating my junior year in high school. Four years and one breakup later, we were still at it. Everyone considered us the perfect couple. She was the complete opposite of me. She was all that was good and pure in my eyes. She was also extremely patient with me. She should have left me years ago.

To my dismay, she told me she had other plans. To drive up would have interrupted her night out in New Orleans, and she'd already told her friends she would go. I thought maybe I had done something wrong, that it was my fault, and as it turned out, I was right. She hated me for volunteering for this war. She thought I was abandoning her and that this would change everything. Well, I wasn't trying to abandon her, but there's no doubt that this changed it all. It was then that I realized I was only human. I was alone, and I had mixed feelings of anger and sadness because of it. I felt betrayed, but all I could do was build up my wall and try to never let it happen again.

The previous week brought the capture of Sadam Hussien, but that weekend would bring nothing. Heartbroken, maybe, I don't know, I just packed my shit and prepared for the long flight ahead of me. A huge barracks' wrestling match would end our stay on Fort Polk. Thanks to Wild Bill and the refueling section, the three-man medical team was protected. When the motor pool came after us during the wrestling match, Wild Bill met them with a gang of men harder than coffin nails. I forgot to thank the refuelers for that. Early the next morning, long before anyone could recover, we were on our way to the airport. It was time for me to get the hell out of this country, and I couldn't say I was all broken up about it.

The fifteen-hour plane ride to Germany was crammed with personnel, our equipment issue, and our weapons. It was anything but enjoyable. By the time we landed, everyone could use a good stretch and a cigarette. Since the military had their own section of the airport, finding a drink was out of the question. After the break, while we were waiting to board the plane again, I found myself standing by Chip, the captain of our company.

Chip: early 30s, 5'5" - VLA Status: Top Priority Enemy. Morals: Low. Chip was VLA's biggest problem in our direct chain of command. The only thing bigger than his list of fuckups was his Napoleon complex. He went out of his way to be an asshole to the enlisted. Fact is, after he reads this book, he'll probably be one of two who will try to pick charges back up against me. Throwing me in prison was one of his goals at the end of our tour.

Since he looked sad, I figured I'd cheer him up.

"They're really taking this annual training thing serious, huh, sir?"

"What are you talking about?"

"You know, making this airport look like it's in Germany. The signs, the cars, they even got actors to act German. They're good. They are good... So, where do you think we really are?" I said, winking and smiling at him.

"This is Germany, and we really are going to Iraq. You all better start taking this shit seriously."

Giggling like a schoolboy who just heard his teacher curse, I countered, "Iraq, that's a good one, sir. You always could make me laugh. Listen, if they end these theatrics early enough, I'm gonna get some of the guys to meet me at the strip club. You can join us if you'd like; should be fun."

The big fake smile was off my face before I could even make it all the way around. If anyone had been close enough to me, they would have heard under my breath, "What a douche bag." But the funny thing was, I think I heard Chip say the same thing under his.

Another ten or so hours on another plane and, by the time I woke up, we were in Kuwait. I remember the feeling as I stepped off the plane. It was as if everything had slowed down; everything, from the wind to the hustling locals, was in slow motion. A feeling came across me that my whole existence was hectic up until this point, that all the worries of everyday life had just gone down the pisser, from my disappointed family, to the bills, all the way to the goals of my life. Everything that I thought was important ceased to exist, and it was a blissful feeling. For the next year, I only had one priority: to survive.

Chapter Three

Hurry Up and Kuwait

Once in Kuwait, the unit gathered under a large, circus-like tent to organize gear, reassemble weapons, and account for personnel. Once again, I found myself in line beside old Chip. As we sat there conversing over some random shit that I can't recall now, the soon-to-be VLA crew took heed. They say that the look on my face made them assume that we were going to kiss, although I doubt it was that bad; it just goes to show that a simple conversation with one of those bastards could end your reputation with the VLA. They ended up busting my balls from that point until I could prove myself once again.

As we reassembled our weapons, Short Stuff, one of our VLA women, realized she had lost the bolt to her M-16.

Short Stuff: 20, 5'4" - VLA Status: Member. Morals: Medium. Short Stuff was a little rough around the edges. She cursed like a dying pirate and loved her liquor just as much. She had a lot more in common with the guys than just the obvious. She was considered a good soldier throughout our tour, but she always resented Chip for the actions he took against her in Kuwait.

The bolt is about the size of a roll of quarters, and it's what makes the weapon sing and dance. Although it is important, it is easily replaceable, and it was the girl's first screw-up ever. A stern talking-to and maybe some tower guard duty would have sufficed; instead, oh merciless Chip decided she would wear full battle gear day and night with her weapon tied to her, for our entire stay in Kuwait. Not that this was an unusual punishment, but he did forget to give himself the same punishment when he lost his own weapon. This sort of hypocrisy was the sunshine for our blooming organization. As long as the shit rolled downhill, it had to collect somewhere; all we did was put our stamp on that location, and we grew.

From our landing point to Camp Wolverine was about a two-hour bus ride. Camp Wolverine was an isolated base when we arrived, but it soon thrived with the hustling and bustling of new units setting up a staging area to move into Iraq. It was our first real chance to coincide with other units. Regular Army, Army Reserves, and the Marine Corp, we all used this base to armor vehicles, train for convoy warfare, and get to know the Iraqi culture. We began to get used to walking blind through sandstorms, taking cold showers, and waiting in two-hour lines for lunch. Actually, we didn't get used to waiting in lines until the marines showed up. Apparently, marines are trained to kill and wait in lines. If one marine stopped to tie his shoe, before he stood up there would be a line of fifty behind him and more charging his way. Other than waiting behind the marines, the cafeteria was top-notch.

The showers, on the other hand, were a different story. They were cold enough to make your balls go bye; I just avoided them completely. I wouldn't take a shower until someone with authority made me. It wasn't just that it was cold, but someone in our unit decided to leave his mark in whichever shower stall he used that night. That's right, the famed shower shitter. What kind of man needs cold water rushing across his body to do his business? Certainly, the kind of man who enjoys golden showers and scat films and any other type of grotesque northern Russian rituals. I don't know where it originated, I'm just saying. Anyway, the men in our unit began to narrow down the suspects until they came up with one name.

Master Sgt.: mid 50s, 5'9" -VLA Status: Neutral-Morals: Medium. The master sergeant was one in a long line of E-8s, and he was extremely cool. He ran through about three or four wives before he vowed never to marry again. He was the oldest pussy hound I've ever met, and the whole crew admired him for it.

Although it can't be proven as fact, I'm pretty sure that sick old bastard was more than capable. Hell, I'm just surprised he didn't start shitting in other people's rucksacks. That's what kind of sickness we were dealing with.

Our living situation was a little better: eighty men and women living under one tent, cots one foot away from each other with gear in between. My cot was set up between Big Vin and DH3. Other than the normal quasi-homosexual activity that men think to be funny, we were usually only in the tent for sleeping, but right before we would sleep, something would happen to all of us. It was as if night brought out some evolutionary link that humanity had forgotten about, a link that made everyone wild animals. At any certain time before lights out, you could stop by any cot and listen to some of the most graphic conversations about girlfriends and boyfriends. Each night, DH3 would have a stripping contest with different female competitors, and the bad thing was that the vote, being ninety percent guys, would always rule in favor of DH3. Before lights out, every night, I would stand in the middle of the tent to pose a question.

"Listen up, anyone bi-curious? Anyone? Alright, have a good night, soldiers."

And when I'd forget they'd remind me. Seriously, some of them sick bastards couldn't go to sleep if I didn't ask. It was considered our Iraqi prayer.

One night in the tent, it got a little more serious. As people were in line to take pictures with Big Vin's grenade links wrapped around their bodies like Rambo, apparently one of the grenades activated itself. Although I'm not sure about this, I think the detonation mechanism is on some sort of swivel. If a grenade is activated, and the mechanism revolves around the swivel thirty times, you would end up explaining to God what you think went wrong. Big Vin didn't know that the grenade was activated and that, just by playing with it, it was turning the mechanism inside. Thank the God that protects idiots that MS High Speed, one of our E-8s, came to our tent just to say hello.

MS High Speed: late 40s, 5'6" - VLA Status: Neutral. Morals: High. MS made a name for himself as a know-it-all, not in the smart-ass sense of the word, but as a real, down-to-earth guy who knew his shit. He would give you a straight-up answer to any question about equipment or military doctrine, and if he didn't know the answer he would find it.

When MS picked up the same link of grenades, he felt the mechanism revolve around the swivel. He immediately evacuated the tent and called EOD (Explosive Ordinance Department,

I think). They sent out a specialist to take the grenade, and we went back to shoving dollars into DH3's panties.

The days at Wolverine were somewhat different. We spent most of the first week armoring vehicles. We loaded our floorboards with sandbags and welded iron plates to the undercarriage. It was a false sense of security that made the things uncomfortable to drive and a son of a bitch to pick up women in. The motor pool got the brunt of the work, which made for an unhappy Big Vin. I think out of the two hundred men in our unit, only one knew how to weld.

Bell: 25, 5'9" - VLA Status: Member. Morals: What're Morals? Bell was the kind of guy who would slap you in the nuts and then stick his fingers in your mouth to say hello. I've had to go to his room twice; both times he was expecting me, and both times he answered the door naked. His favorite saying was, "You're not gay if you're giving it. Know what I mean?"

Having to weld armor to the undercarriage of every vehicle in the unit, Bell spent a week on his back, which is probably less time than his girlfriend did back in the states. He single-handedly put every vehicle on line, ready for the convoy.

After the vehicles were armored, Sgt. Maj. began recruiting for a cleanup of the area. Since the guys and I were in the front of our tent, he figured he didn't need to look any farther. He walked us into the open desert parking lot where our vehicles were once staged and told us to make a clean sweep of all the cigarette butts. As I slowly walked the fence line I began putting all the butts that I picked up in my mouth. When we were finished, the sergeant major asked me why I didn't pick up anything. I then spit the wad of butts into my hand and winked at him.

"What the hell is wrong with you, boy? You'd better hope none of those cigarettes have AIDS on 'em," he said, using his deepest hick accent.

Realizing that I had one left in my mouth, I squeezed it between my lips as if I was smoking it and said, "Nothing I ain't got already, Sgt. Major."

By the time Sgt. Maj. started shaking his head, I noticed Giff about five feet away with his nose in the air and his mouth open. So I sucked the butt back in my mouth and spit it into the air. Giff made an amazing catch with his mouth and began chewing the butt himself. Sgt. Maj. wrinkled his forehead in disgust, turned around, and began making his way back to the tent. I did it so that the Sgt. Maj. would second-guess himself before giving me another detail. Giff did it because I think he was neglected as a child.

That night, while I was shaving, AA decided to use the sink onside mine for his own personal grooming efforts. Before noticing that Sgt. Maj. was in one of the shower stalls, we began to talk about our next operation. "Operation Heart Stop" had very simple rules. Any volunteer who joined would put up fifty dollars, which would make him entitled to the pot if he won. No player could call or write letters home. All would be allowed to receive letters or packages from home, but without being able to notify your family with an address where they could reach you, it didn't make sense to expect anything. If any player received and opposed a Red Cross alert (an urgent message that would find you no matter where you were), all other players would put in another fifty dollars. The last player to call home won the pot.

Once again, AA astounded me with his sick ingenuity. As soon as I walked out of the bathroom trailer, I began recruiting. Little did I know that AA was confronted by a soaking-wet Sgt. Maj.

"Son, can you explain those rules to me again?"

And of course AA did.

"But Sgt. Major, if you want to get in this, it's fifty bucks up front."

AA later said that he thought Sgt. Maj. looked like he genuinely wanted in.

The next morning, command called a special formation. They emphasized the importance of family contact and further explained the legal actions that could be taken against gambling in Iraq. Chip ended the formation saying, "I want to see two individuals start walking to the telephone tent after this formation. You know who you are. If you need calling cards, go and see First Sgt."

AA and I immediately fell out and began walking toward the telephone tent. While we were walking, we bitched about the absolute power they had over us. How could they *make* us call our mommy? Seriously? What if we had no one to call? What if our whole family died in some tragic event, like if they were hit by a bus while walking to a telephone tent somewhere? Then they would feel like shit, wouldn't they? Somehow, our bitching turned to plotting, and soon our plotting turned into conspiring. We decided to organize the crew and try our damndest to give them sons a bitches hell, not just for the day, and not just in Kuwait, but for the entirety of the deployment. We figured that maybe they would stop making stupid rules if no one listened to them. Maybe they would take their heads out of their asses if our foot was taking up most of the room. With the crew already in place, and at least a man in each section so as to be completely informed, all we had to do was find a name. With my French background and AA's love for anarchy, we decided to go with Vive La Anarchy (VLA).

Upon our return from the PX or post exchange (like we were going to go make a phone call with all that anarchy talk going on), the unit was preparing to leave Wolverine to make our way to a deserted area of the desert for more combat training. I don't want to say much about this, except it was necessary training and many of the officers, including Chip, didn't go. The officers, of course, were to fly to our Iraqi post in C-130 planes; for this they were excluded from the course.

After we had finished our high-speed, over the tracks training, we returned to Wolverine for our last week of preparations. As I walked back to my tent, I figured I would check with Col. Rock to see if he needed anything, but when I walked into his tent, I noticed all his shit was gone. When I inquired into his whereabouts, the officer in the next cot said he decided to catch an earlier flight headed to Balad. That was him.

"Oh, there's a flight headed to Balad? Well, I'm supposed to go to Balad anyway; might as well get a head start."

He probably didn't even clear it with anyone. This was why we initiated him into VLA, for shit like this. He was the ultimate "screw you" to the chain of command, and with the bird on his collar, they would just have to bend over and take it like men, or so we thought. But sadly, this would be the last time he could use the old, "Oh, I didn't know I couldn't do that." The next time we would all pay.

The command decided to give us the rest of that day off for personal use. Personal time consisted mostly of cleaning. Our laundry was done in water buckets, just add soap, rub together, rinse in a separate bucket, and hang. It was simple, but it took a while. Our weapons seemed to be magnets for the baby-powder sand out there. Hell, I even decided to take my weekly shower. After there was nothing left to clean, I retired to the tent for some wholesome, nonalcoholic Budweiser and some fun. We were told that the next day we were going to map our route in, discuss possible obstacles, and go over the rules of engagement.

When we woke up the next morning, a plan was in place to drop our Humvees off on the other side of the base for some last-minute up-armoring. Somehow, they had pulled some strings to get us hardened doors with bulletproof glass. It all sounded great to me, so I volunteered to drive one of the Humvees there and take the bus back. All was going well until Sgt. Maj. stepped to the back of the bus and asked DH3 to step to the front so he could have a word with me. Now, although the rule of thumb is never to align yourself with any form of the command, the proposal that he had was a tempting one. Apparently, he had found out from some of the girls in the female barracks that not only did Sgt. LT. have liquor at Fort Polk, but she called ahead of the sweep, and she had me hide hers. He continued explaining that he didn't agree with how she was running things and claimed he knew that I felt the same. Then he dropped the offer on me.

"Now, if you want her gone, all you have to do is make a statement, and I'll take this thing as far as it'll go."

This is why you can't bring women into conspiracies. They can't keep their go'damn mouths shut. Instead of blackmailing her until the statute of limitations was up, the girls from the barracks had to run and tell the first person with authority. Don't get me wrong, there was no doubt it would have made it easier for me to be rid of her. Maybe they would have put Mic G in charge, but I wanted to do it on my terms, no one else's.

"Sorry, Sgt. Maj., I have no clue what you're talking about."

And he left it at that. Since Knight Ryder was the bus driver and had seen the whole event unfold, I decided to try to spin it. I went to Sgt. LT. with Knight Ryder as my witness and told her that Sgt. Maj. was gunning for her. I told her everything that had happened, even at the cost of me looking like a kiss-ass. She listened intently and at the end said, "Thanks, I owe you one."

That statement was as good as an IOU from a crack head. I would never see the return on it; instead, she would try to hang me at every turn. Who could blame her? She was practically giving an

IOU to a man on death row because soon I wouldn't have enough credibility to harm a soul.

After lunch that day, we began to watch videos of roadside bombs, suicide bombers, and I think they might've thrown in some of the Hiroshima film for laughs. They scared the shit out of everyone who was there to witness it. As if people weren't scared enough, now you had to prove to them that the armor on their vehicles was just for show. They had most of the kids petrified, and they looked like they were having fun doing it, so I decided to have a little fun myself. For the remainder of the day, I walked around with an empty notebook, stopping random people in my unit. As I flipped through my hand-size notebook, I decided, with no rhyme or reason, who was going to make it through the convoy and who should write their last will and testament. "Ah, Hamp, congratulations. It looks like you're going to make it through the convoy. I'll see you in Balad. Hold on, *esse*, let me find your name. Torres…Torres…Torres, oh here you are. Amigo, if I were you, I'd make my peace with whatever God looks after you Mexicans. It doesn't look like you're going to survive. I'm sorry. I guess God stops protecting you once you get past border patrol."

Most of the guys thought it was funny; some met it with a "screw you," but one took it to heart. One of the women, unhappy to know that her end was coming shortly, decided to bring her quarrel straight to my vowed enemy. When Chip made eye contact with me, I knew something was wrong. He began shaking his head and clenching his teeth as he turned his stroll into a full step. With his short little legs, it was sometimes hard to tell the difference, but I've been around him long enough to know.

"What the hell is wrong with you? Please tell me that you are not telling people that they're going to die on the convoy. Please tell me that!"

"Sir, it's not like I'm wishing death on anyone. If it's your time to go, it's your time to go."

"This is not a fucking joke; you better go and apologize to that female by the tent over there, and be thankful that I don't have your ass for this."

"Sir, is this all because you found out that you're on the 'will perish' list? I mean, I can take you off. It's not going to change your destiny, but…"

"Get out of my sight. I'll talk to your first sergeant, and we'll decide what to do with you."

As soon as he turned around, I knew nothing was going to come of it, but I did feel I should apologize to the female. I mean, really, I didn't want her to die mad at me.

Forty eight hours later brought the day of the convoy; it was time to separate the men from whatever we were. The morning was apparently already blissful for Mic G. As Knight Ryder and I were overlooking our war chariots, he approached with a good sign. Supposedly, he and Sgt. LT. turned the go-can into a scene from *Deep Throat* before sunrise. I took this as a sign of two things to come. The first was that the medical section would make it through the convoy without a hitch. The second was that Sgt. LT. would lower the number of soldiers in Iraq by half when they all had to show up for a Jerry Springer's "Don't know who my baby daddy is" edition. I was wrong about both.

Just as we were putting our vehicles into the convoy line, Chip showed up to let us know to be careful, be agile, and be observant. He told us that he was going to worry about us, but he had no doubt that we were all going to make it, and he had complete faith in our abilities as soldiers. Then the commander showed up to let him know that he was going to be joining us on the convoy because there was no more room on the plane. At that point, he should have begun running around screaming, "We're all going to die!" and only stopped long enough to dig a hole and put his head in it, because his eyes were telling the whole story. The way he looked is the way I'm sure most people looked when they were told the Twin Towers had been hit. I didn't know whether to laugh or cry, but now I know I should've cried until I was dehydrated and made them fly me over what would soon be a ten-second clip on the Channel 6 News.

From Wolverine to the Iraqi border was going to take the rest of the day. Everyone was pretty laid-back before movement, still laughing and joking, maybe even missing the place already. We didn't know if we should be this relaxed, but one thing was for sure, some were more relaxed than others. When the clock had reached the departure time, a voice came over the radio explaining that we were missing personnel and the departure time would be pushed back five mikes (minutes). Fifteen mikes later, our two missing personnel returned...with ice cream. Chip and his driver, the lieutenant, missed movement to fetch some ice cream cones from the cafeteria.

The Lieutenant: mid 30s, 6'1" - VLA Status: Neutral. Morals: Medium. The Lieutenant was a lapdog for Chip and the first sergeant. The only reason he held neutral status is because he was completely harmless. He would inquire into everything, and it became a good rule of thumb to lie to him. You could be assured that your misinformation would get to the command.

Now, I'm not here to judge, because I could have used a nice cold ice cream cone myself, But are you kidding me? Missing movement is a serious offence. This should have been met with harsh punishment; instead, I didn't hear another thing about it. Maybe The Lieutenant brought Sgt. Maj. one too. I don't know. I do know this: if I had received one, maybe a chocolate/vanilla swirl, this chapter would have been a paragraph shorter.

Chapter Four

Convoy: Like a Conga Line, but with More Idiots

Within the first couple of hours, everyone had gotten used to the speeding locals, dodging oncoming cars that were in the wrong lane, and broken-down Mercedes that had just been left on the interstate. Being from New Orleans, we figured it wasn't much different than driving during Mardi Gras. Even the gun barrels hanging out of each side of the vehicles reminded us of home. Sgt. LT. and I were placed in the second vehicle of the first chalk. I was driving, of course. Even in Iraq, it's dangerous to let a woman drive. Our medical counterparts, Mic G and Knight Ryder, were placed in the second vehicle in the second chalk (a chalk is a group of twenty to thirty vehicles). Although the chalks were only separated by fifteen minutes, it would be very unlikely that any of the three were going to meet, and more disastrously, that any one chalk could get to the other if trouble arose.

Trouble was the last thing on my mind, though. I hadn't talked to Hollie since I left Fort Polk. The flask filled with VO in my pocket reminded me of her. We had bought it together in a New Orleans mall. I was wondering what she was doing, if she was thinking about me, if I were to die how long would it take her to replace me. Although time stops for us, back home everyone carries on. They go on with their lives meeting new people, experiencing new things, while all along we just want them to sit by the phone waiting for us to call, revolving everything around the date of our return. It's a sad life of a soldier and a sad life for the people who love us. I also hadn't spoken to anyone in my family, but I was sure that everyone was fine and maybe I would call them when I arrived at Balad.

When we arrived at the border of Kuwait and Iraq, we were surprised to see a nice little setup. The little base there was equipped with a first-class cafeteria, warm showers, and even a little PX. As we parked in a staging area to the west of all the amenities, the chaplain approached my door.

Chaplain: late 50s, 5'9" - VLA Status: Supporter. Morals: High. A chaplain is a man of God for soldiers. It would be a disservice to say that all he did was hold Mass on Sunday. He traveled from base to base risking his own life to serve the men and women of the war with God's word. He brought a sense of comfort to the killing; he tried to keep men sane in an insane place. He supported VLA in the sense that a soldier must do whatever he has to do to keep his mind off this mission.

Knowing that I was an atheist, he jumped at every chance possible to talk to me. On this particular occasion, he inquired into the assembly and disassembly of an M-16. I told him that I carried a SAW (Squad Automatic Weapon), so I would show him how to assemble it instead. He then surprised me by saying, "Well, my assistant carries an M-16, and if, God forbid, anything should happen to him, an M-16 would be the only thing within reach."

Holy shit, a warrior chaplain! I guess what they say is right. There are no conscientious objectors when the bullets start flying. I proudly agreed to help him and called for Big Vin to come and see me. He handed me his M-16 with full confidence and joined his section for a meeting. I disassembled it while explaining, in detail, each piece as the chaplain listened closely. Upon reassembly, I noticed that the firing pin was missing. I frantically began to search the Humvee and the ground for the pencil-tip-sized piece. The chaplain and Big Vin joined me to no avail. After an hour and a half of looking, we decided to give up. I would have easily given him my firing pin, but the SAW and the M-16 do not have interchangeable parts. Vinny put his face in his hands, showing a sign of hopelessness. When he looked up, I'll never forget what he said.

"One day we're gonna laugh about this, but it sure as fuck ain't today."

I felt horrible, but probably not as bad as he felt. In twelve hours he'd be entering Iraq with a weapon that didn't work. God dam, I felt horrible, I told him to join me for lunch and I would buy him something from the PX. A very little consolation for a tremendous fuckup, but Big Vin took me up on it and we began to walk and bullshit.

When we made it inside the cafeteria, Big Vin hit the salad bar and hit it hard; he was on a constant mission to lose weight. On the other hand, I had whatever fried foods they had to serve. We ate and talked over the next day's route. We speculated on any attacks that might come and what we thought we would do in the face of danger, knowing all along we hadn't a clue. When we finished up there, we made our way to the PX where, lo and behold, we found our unit's administration sergeant.

Admin. Sgt.: mid 30s, 5'10" - VLA Status: Awesome physique. Morals: I wish they were lower. Admin. Sgt. was in charge of the unit's administrative section and was known as a bitch to her soldiers, but I never saw her as a problem. She was very professional but would sway just enough to flirt with me. She was a light-skinned black woman who was in the running for the best looking in our unit.

She was four soldiers behind Big Vin and I, and I figured it wouldn't take her long to catch up if we walked slow. Instead, I decided to send Big Vin ahead while I waited for her. Big Vin just smiled and shook his head. As she came out the door, I took her bags and we started back to the staging area. She was interested in my "don't give a shit" attitude, and I was interested in what she could teach me that the rest of the eighteen-year-olds girls couldn't. As we talked, I came to the realization that she didn't want a soldier's life any more than I did. She was too close to retirement to give up, and it gave her a chance to get away from the husband. A year away from the husband might seem like a little much, but apparently they were having problems, and she just happened to throw that in. I liked her and would continue to like her and defend her throughout Iraq. When we got to the staging area, we split up quickly, due to eager eyes and loud mouths.

We would spend the rest of the night in our Humvees. I seriously doubt anyone got good sleep. First, the anticipation of breaking the border was on everyone's mind, and second, the Kuwait nights are colder than a witch's tit. By the time 4:00 a.m. rolled around, everyone had brushed their teeth and was ready to roll. Since I was in the first chalk, I didn't have to wait long before the reality set in.

"First chalk, move out!"

I had pictured this moment from the time they activated our unit. Bombs exploding, guns blaring, people yelling, "Medic!", all the fury and chaos that is warfare after passing a single sign, "You are now entering Iraq." What we found on the other side of the border did depict chaos, chaos that had happened six months earlier or maybe even in '89, broken up roads, blown up tanks, a people that just wanted to stay the hell away from us. It oddly reminded me of the U.S., but after some sort of apocalypse. The interstates had the same glowing green signs; you could see cities in the background; they even had English translations on the street corners. The people could easily be described as different. In the south, it was all nomads; you would see a family in front of a Jeep-sized mud hut, but nothing else, nothing around them but a hundred miles of sand. I couldn't fathom how these people got here or lived here. I didn't see any water or livestock or form of transportation. They were just there. I didn't understand it then, but before my tour was up, I would become one myself.

While I was enjoying the sights of a new world, Sgt. LT. was going over call signs and a map that might as well have been written on a bar napkin. We were paying attention to any approaching vehicle, as we were trained to do, when Sgt. LT. excused herself to use the bathroom. That's pretty much the nicest way I could explain going to the bathroom in a moving Humvee while driving through a war zone. They apparently issued some sort of device that made it easy for women to do this. It looked like a rubber athlete's cup with a two-foot hose funneling to wherever. As she put her hand on my shoulder for balance, I couldn't help but think that some people pay good money for this type of shit; hell, I'm sure Master Sgt. would have. I also began to think that the Army was no democracy. They could give a shit less if you didn't feel comfortable pissing a foot away from a soldier of the opposite sex. They didn't care if you would prefer a female gynecologist, or a male checking for hernias. We were not in the land of preference anymore. With saying that, I took the oil drip pan, put it between my legs, and took a piss myself. While Mic G got the cool nickname of *Beast Master*, she also bestowed me with a nickname: *Least Master.* Just kidding. We were fresh out of shyness; all we had left was crude and raw.

Before nightfall, we made it to the halfway point without a scratch. It looked like there were about two dozen units that made it there before us. We were all staging there before we entered the infamous Sunni Triangle. That day, we learned that there were many units that took the same supply route, which was probably the reason we didn't run into any trouble. When I started comparing maps with these other units, I realized that they were all breaking off towards Baghdad, so further north of our next day's journey would be done alone. It wasn't very reassuring, but what other option did we have?

Again, the next morning came early. We left before daybreak and were nearing the west side of Baghdad for lunch when a voice came over the radio. It was our chalk commander calling back to the second chalk commander with doubts about the map. It seemed we had taken the wrong exit, and he was asking if they did the same. Well, since they hadn't passed that exit yet, they decided to join us, so that we would all be lost in the middle of Baghdad. The third chalk commander didn't want to be left out and decided to descend on Baghdad as well. Now, we were all lost in the middle of terrorist country, but our chalk commander had one more trick up his sleeve. He decided to do a U-turn in the middle of a packed street to make our way back to the interstate. This road, not being like an American interstate, had no on-ramp returning to the interstate. Now, trying to figure out where everyone was, the commanders were screaming directions back and forth. We were separated, lost, and thought that it couldn't get any worse. At that point, I and many other people saw a middle-aged man on the side of the road counting vehicles as they passed. He wasn't trying to hide it; in fact, it looked like he was auditioning for the Count on Sesame Street. Then a voice screeched over the radio. "Contact right! Contact right!"

"Contact right" means someone is getting attacked from the right side. Sgt. LT. and I scanned our perimeters and our mirrors to see if we had a visual. Nothing. Our chalk commander called back.

"Which chalk? Which chalk is under attack?"

Nothing. While we were going through radio silence, the second chalk was going through hell.

On the next street, a couple of miles back, some jihad fuck rolled a grenade in front of Topp's vehicle.

Topp: mid 40s, 6'0" - VLA Status: Neutral. Morals: Medium. Topp was the most well-informed man in our unit. He made it his business to know what everyone was doing at all times, not that he ever tried to stop us. He was as laid-back as Jamaica and twice as cool. He always told VLA that there was a right way to do a wrong thing.

Luckily, his driver had come to a stop because of the crowd. Topp would later say that the road peeled back and resembled a wave at the beach. After that, the smoke covered everything. They began driving blind with one vehicle following them. Only his and another vehicle made it past the kill zone; the other vehicle was the ambulance with Knight Ryder and Mic G in it. They recall that the rear gunner of Topp's vehicle was down; they could see he was face down in the bed of the Humvee. Without being able to slow down Topp's vehicle and with communication out, Mike decided to jump from the ambulance into the bed of Topp's truck, it was the kind of shit you see in a movie. As soon as Mic G pulled up close enough and Knight Ryder opened his door to make his way to the hood of the humvee, the rear gunner stood to his feet. With a breath of relief, Mic G fell back, and the rear gunner stared at them for a second...then broke into the air guitar. Fucking rockstars.

I couldn't say the same for the rest of chalk two. It seems the third vehicle in the chalk took command. In this vehicle was a man who hadn't attended convoy training; in fact, he didn't even know he was going to be in the convoy until two days before, but that wouldn't stop Chip; it was his time to shine. With his extensive training, he decided to circle the wagons. Circling the wagons is an old west term for bringing the vehicles into a circle and forming a barrier from which the men could fight. It was a beautiful plan to the untrained eye, and that's exactly what he had. The rest of his men knew that, with an obvious exit route, the protocol was to beat feet and shoot anything looking suspicious. So now, as Chip was trying to get the men out of their vehicles, he was relieved of his command by a young black sergeant driving a fuel truck.

Don Perignon: late 20s, 5'7" - VLA Status: Member. Morals: Medium. Don Perignon would gain a name for himself from monopolizing the sex-toy market. He was a laid-back leader of the refuelers who helped out with everything from black-market deals to breaking into the black community.

Supposedly, the young fueler listened to his instincts and blew Chip off like a Chinese ladyboy. As he took the exit route through the smoke, the rest of the men followed; eventually, Chip was forced to fall in line and follow a VLA member out of the danger.

As chalk one arrived at the front gate of Balad Airfield, Topp and the other medics were leaving. They had arrived before us and were now moving out again to find the rest of their chalk. Instead of cowering in a corner with their tails between their legs, they were going back out into the chaos to pull their boys in by the hair. They were making adult decisions, but I would be lying if I said I didn't envy them. That day, it seemed that they were on a mission from God. It gives me chills thinking about it now.

When Topp finally arrived, we had a chance to check him and his driver out; they suffered some minor lacerations with possible damage to the ear. His rear gunner was also diagnosed with possible damage to the ear. Our boys in medicine were unscathed in the second vehicle. We made it with a one hundred percent survival rate and few injuries. Some men had stories to go home and tell their families, and some just got to go home; either way, I was stoked. We survived the city; now let's see if the city can survive us. As we rolled onto base, I set my weapon aside, leaned back in my seat, and took a swig from my flask while Sgt. LT. yelled. We were home, and the only way we were leaving within the next year was in a body bag.

Chapter Five

Drunk Again in Mortaritaville

Mortaritaville was the name given to Balad by someone in Operation Iraqi Freedom 1, mainly because this place had more mortar round attacks than any other base in Iraq, but I took it as a sign from God. He was telling me, "Find liquor, get drunk." That's what I like about God, he always has the simplest plans, you know.

"God, how do we get to the promised land?"

"Fuck, I don't know, Moses. Walk through the desert for forty years. After that, I'm sure you'll be thankful for any place you come across."

I would follow God's instructions to the T, but thinking back on it, maybe it wasn't God's instructions after all.

Upon arrival, we were called to a formation. Prior to formation the men stood around conversing over the earlier happenings. The chalk commanders were all there. They were being completely up-front with what had happened, and I might even venture to say they were being a little apologetic. Even Topp, face still cut up, was saying what a disaster it was. We were all just thankful to be alive. Then thankful turned to angry when Chip took the forefront of the formation. What began spewing out of his mouth was a story that was obviously from an alternate universe, a universe where he heroically and single-handedly led the men out of harm's way. In this universe, he obviously didn't look like an ass in front of all the men, but in our universe the real story was already known, and his speech made it funnier. I didn't mind it; in fact, I figured he'd do something like that, but what I did mind was that Topp or any of the other chalk commanders didn't backhand him. I realized then that these men of power weren't trying to make any waves; they just wanted to get to their retirement. Everyone just wanted to get to retirement.

After the formation, we were to acquire a set of keys to small, two-man rooms. My roommate was to be Fitz Gerald.

Fitz Gerald: 30, 5'6" - VLA Status: Member. Morals: Medium High. Gerald was the chaplain's assistant and would do anything for that man. He was moody at best, but he was always in the inner circle of our enemies. He was all the entertainment we would ever need in one man, singing, impersonation, and most definitely drama. He was the furthest from my best friend, but he was the only one who knew who I really was.

As I and my already chosen roommate stood in line for our set, I noticed that your name was written by the room in which you were assigned, but there was no process in place to check if you had a room already. What I'm trying to say is that they knew which rooms were taken, but nothing else. Theoretically, one man could occupy many rooms. The number I occupied would grow with each story told, but I think the truth was somewhere around eleven rooms. Whenever it would get hot, I would just jump ship.

That night, Gerald and I shared life stories over the remainder of VO in my flask. He seemed to be a very down-to-earth guy with his goals in sight, marriage, a house, a six-figure job with a stay-at-home wife. I should have known then that I was only going to be a bad influence on him. On the other hand, on that first night, he attained more information about me than anyone would for the rest of the tour. Within two hours, he concluded that I wasn't as hard as I seemed, and I was actually just a heartbroken, scared little twenty-one-year-old. He deciphered the lies and called them for the exact truths that they were. He knew more about me than I did, and I hated him for it. It was too hot already, time for me to jump ship.

The next day, the medics reported to the hospital (if you would like to see it you could watch *Baghdad ER*) to meet the other medical personnel from the other units. Everyone seemed cool. We even had a dental office...with a good-looking dentist and her good-looking assistant. Work we loved, good people to do it with, and something to look at. I couldn't ask for more. Except one thing was missing, where the hell was Col. Rock? They told me in Kuwait that he was already here, and when I got here they gave me a different story. Apparently, he had taken one look at the clinic and decided that we needed more up-to-date equipment. He then jumped on the next thing smoking towards Manhiem, Germany, where our main critical care and surgical hospital was, to bargain for better hospital efforts. Things like this would continue to gain him respect within the ranks, but to a control freak commander, he had just signed his death warrant.

We continued without him for the next two weeks, but it wouldn't stop me from making new friends.

Arilious: 24, 5'7" - VLA Status: Officer. Morals: Low. Arilious shared the same building as the hospital. He was the legal advisor to the unit and the illegal advisor to the VLA. The command had to notify Arilious if they were going to take any legal action. Room searches, Article 15s, and even drug tests were passed by Arilious' desk at least two days prior.

Arilious was only two doors down from me. He had spent two years in Korea on active duty and knew the ins and outs of the military. From first glance, one would think he was too smart to be in the Army, but being under the legal radar while being on top of an illegal organization is where he shined. Over the next year, he would become one of two men I trusted. He was so loyal he would almost be dragged into the depths of destruction before it was all over.

During our evenings off, the VLA would gather between two pods, or living quarters in a space that would become known as "Motor City" or "Mo-town." I think Big Vin came up with the name. The two trailers included six rooms with four VLA officers, and the rest all members. We would talk about the day's events and the prospective women. Sometimes, we would even get into conversations about back home, which would diminish to nothing once the import of liquor started. We were soldiers doing our mission, not making waves, helping out in every way possible, then one day at our gathering The Lieutenant showed up. He pulled me aside from the antics and told me to report to Topp immediately. I had a mission.

Topp's office was a mile away. During my walk, I couldn't help but think they had finally found a use for me. Treating flu-like symptoms and depression was starting to get old. Yeah, even after a couple of weeks. I thought maybe Topp saw some talent, but I was only disappointed to see AA standing in the office where I was supposed to be. Now I figured we were in trouble. Who knew what they had on us, and by the look on AA's face, he thought the same. Finally, when Topp emerged from his office he didn't waste any time.

"You two report to the Mississippi unit. Ya'll are on tower guard this week."

How I was chosen, I don't know. How we were chosen together, there was definetly crack involved.

Tower guard is the occupation, by friendly forces, of elevated towers strategically placed around a base for the protection of the personnel inside, and I don't even have a dictionary. The mission wasn't a bullshit one, and in my unit that's pretty much all I could ask for. We reported to an office that was in the same building as the hospital as instructed, and there we met the sergeant of the guard. I can't remember her name, but she was a "nine" by desert ranking, probably a "six" back in the states.

Desert Ranking - Desert ranking was a system that assisted men in coming to terms with the laying of ugly women. The desert ranking system took into consideration the lack of heterosexual, beautiful women in theatre and then ranked appropriately. Any woman could be applied to a scale from one to ten, ten being the most beautiful. If the case may be that a girl in the United States was ranked as a six, that same girl in Iraq would be a ten.

As we went over the upcoming mission, she explained, in a Mississippi twang, that we would be on tower for four hours and off for eight. For the next week, AA and I expected an easy ride. We shot off some flares and shot a dog that was trying to dig a hole under the fence. We talked about everything from the weather to our overall mission out there. After a week, we decided that we couldn't do much good with our unit; they were kitty cats wrapped in vagina cloth, and we were hungry for action. We decided to approach Task Force Tacomba with an offer.

Task Force Tacomba (TFT): Tacomba was the base's security force made up of volunteers from various units. They patrolled the outer perimeter of the base and enforced curfew in the surrounding towns.

The first sergeant of TFT decided that if our unit would approve, I could start immediately as the team's medic, and if they needed another, they would contact AA. AA was torn; being a light wheel mechanic, he wasn't a real necessity to an active security sect. I felt bad but continued to my command.

"If you call your family and tell them that I'm not the reason you're going to get your ass blown off, then go right ahead. I'll even talk to Sgt. Maj. for you."

I figured Chip would say that; he wanted nothing more than to get rid of me, and there he went again telling me to call my family. I'm glad he had to check with his mother every time he squatted to take a piss, but I didn't.

I volunteered for another week on the tower so that they could get used to not seeing me while they made the decision to let me go. AA returned to the motor pool, and now I was stuck with some douche bag from a Florida unit. I made it through the week until my second-to-last day. Our four-hour shift turned into eight, and soon our com set (radio) started getting chatter. It wasn't just us who was stuck out there, but the whole thirty man strong tower detail. A soldier from the base's security unit had finally come out to apologize and explained that the sergeant of the guard didn't send out our replacements. After two consecutive night shifts of fighting off bugs and fatigue, I didn't want to hear anything the sergeant of the guard had to say when I returned, but she knew how to catch my attention.

"Excuse me, specialist, I don't have anyone to replace my guards for next shift, so if you all could stick around for the next four hours, you all are going to take the next shift."

"Listen, hun, we just did eight hours out there; let them do the same."

"I can't, the people that are out there now aren't supposed to be out there. I had to round them up out of bed."

"Well, that's your fucking problem," I said, turning to the crowd of tower guards with me. "Listen up, meet me back here in eight hours. We still have another shift to do. Have a good night."

"Specialist!" she interjected

"Darlin', if you have anything else, send whoever is in charge of you to the hospital. That's where I'll be."

I felt like I was doing a justice for the lower enlisted who wouldn't speak up for themselves, and even with a sergeant yelling over my shoulder, they took my word. It felt good to realize that rank wasn't depicted by an emblem on someone's collar but in a person and his or her actions. As I walked down the hall toward the hospital, I turned back to see if she was pissed. She wasn't; she was crying. Just like every one of us, she was frustrated to the point of breaking down. I started to think of the madness she had gone through that night. I turned around and ran out the door. When I opened it, I shouted, "Everybody be back here in four hours, four hours!"

I stood there for a second to hear voices passing the message. I then turned around and noticed the little girl's half smile.

"Get your shit together, honey; this is a one-time thing."

"How do you know they'll come back?"

"They'll come back, believe me." I closed the door to the hospital and lay in one of the empty beds.

Hell, I didn't know if they would come back. If it had been me, I wouldn't have, but sure enough, four hours later there was one hundred percent accountability. It felt good; things were starting to look up for me.

The next day was my last on tower guard. When I returned I reported to Sgt. Maj. to find out the verdict.

"Specialist, I do appreciate you trying to do all you can, but the fact of the matter is that we're trying to make this tour as safe as possible. We're not going to put anyone in harm's way if we don't have to. We have to think about the families back home. Now, in a couple months, when everything is settled down, then maybe we can try this thing again, but as for right now, I'm going to have to say no."

There it was, my mission was flight physicals and sunburns for the rest of the tour. I was pissed, but there wasn't really anything I could do. I decided to take the next day off; things were so unorganized that Sgt. LT. just thought I was still on tower guard. When I woke up for a late breakfast the next morning, Col. Rock was sitting by his lonesome at one of the tables in the dining facility. He was definitely a sight for sore eyes. While we ate, we talked about tower guard and Task Force Tacomba. We walked through his trip to Germany. If I can remember correctly, I think he brought back damn near thirty thousand dollars worth of medical equipment. He was a go'damn miracle worker, and he should have been praised. That's when his praise showed up.

The Colonel: mid 40s, 5'10" - VLA Status: Enemy. Morals: Medium High. The colonel was in charge of the entire unit. He was a tough son of a bitch. Prided himself in karate. Once he walked straight up to the hospital with a ruptured appendix. He was a control freak, and he protected Chip; both would make him an enemy of VLA.

The Colonel appeared at the head of the table and requested to have a word with Col. Rock in private. They then took their pissing contest outside. What happened there was told to me by Col. Rock. Supposedly, as they walked outside, The Colonel began to question Col. Rock about his unauthorized trip to Germany; then Col. Rock interrupted and insisted that The Colonel begin any conversation with a higher ranking officer with a salute. The Colonel then saluted him and carried on with trying to intimidate Col. Rock with threats. Through the conversation, The Colonel realized that it was obvious that Col. Rock wouldn't be intimidated. The Colonel then explained that he had made some provisions for Col. Rock to be transferred to Africa for a peace-keeping mission. To Africa, with a snap of the finger, he sent my only reason for staying straight to Africa. It made me sick to my stomach.

I agreed to help Col. Rock pack, and then I went to my room for the rest of the morning. I just lay there to let it all soak in. This thing was crumbling down around me. The command was just too powerful; they weren't going to reason, they didn't care why he went to Germany, and they certainly didn't give a shit what I thought. I figured I had nothing to lose anyway, so I went and volunteered to go to Africa with Col. Rock; they refused of course, and I helped him pack. While we were packing, Col. Rock started bawling; I felt bad enough to cry myself. He offered to go to the command and request that I go with him once again. He did, and they refused again. He wasn't exactly the toughest, and now he had no one to watch his back. The last thing he said to me when he was walking out the door was, "Don't take any shit from them bastards, and promise me you're going to take care of yourself." Both of us were trying to hold tears back. I made the promise, and I tried to keep it as long as I could, but like I said, they were just too powerful.

Later that evening, I decided to call home; this would be the first of only a handful of phone calls I would make. Hollie's parents answered. If I would have called before, I would have known that she had taken a vacation in Vegas with her college roommate. It would be another week before she returned. Alone again, I had only been there for a month or two, and I was close to breaking. I realized that it wouldn't help to flip out now; some of the men there depended on me to be the "nobody gives a shit, stick together and we'll make it" type of guy. If they knew that I was having my period, there would have been a lot of men out there on the rag. I guess it's like the menstrual cycle of female roommates; if one of us was pissed, then we were all on the verge of a revolution, but if one of us could keep a straight head, then all of us were pretty mellow. I sucked it up and carried on.

I went through a couple of weeks at the hospital, doing my job, listening to people complain, thinking to myself that not one of these soldiers would make it outside of these gates, that most of these people should be at home watching the war on TV like everyone else. It made me sick that no matter what I tried I couldn't participate more; I couldn't do what I came here to do. To think that you gave away a year of your life to make history, and all that would come of it was post-traumatic stress disorder. I just wanted to go home and make history on my own. I missed Hollie more than ever. I figured she was the only one hurting as much as I, that as much as I felt alone, she felt the same. I figured she was home by this time, so I decided to give her a call.

When she answered the phone, I almost starting crying, but I was using the phone in the sergeant of the guard's office and I didn't want her to come in and see me crying.

"Hey, hun, it's good to hear your voice."

"Oh, I'm glad you remembered having a girlfriend." It sounded like she was about to cry.

"I remember; I'm sorry. I've been busy."

Then she started bawling. "I have to tell you something."

"What is it, babe?"

"I went to Las Vegas last week with Katie, and we got real drunk. Then I met a guy, and we were drinking and..."

"Hollie, Hollie, Hollie, I don't have time for this shit...this is what I need you to do, I need you to finish school. And then...then I'll see you in a year or so. I have to go."

I was out of breath as if I had run four miles. I had lost all control of everything in my life, and I couldn't pinpoint when it had started going downhill. I was under a regime that wouldn't let me piss without calling my mother; they stole the glory of war, they stole the only man I would lift a finger for, and now this shit. I just couldn't see the light at the end of the tunnel. I didn't want to leave that dark corner. I wanted to sit there staring at the phone until the war was over, or until my grandmother came out of the next room with soup...and hookers. Well, I think my grandmother was late, because the hooker showed up; the sergeant of the guard walked in. Many people after this point would ask what the hell happened to me, as a soldier, as a man, as a human fucking being. Well, this was it. This is where the road turned; this is where I stopped trying to be a leader, a hero, and anything that resembled family. I decided that I would do my thing; whether people followed was up to them. The sorrowing feeling subsided.

"Hey, how long until the changing of the guard?"

"Auh, about two hours." she replied, the Mississippi twang getting sexier now.

"Come meet me. I'll be in the clinic."

"Excuse me?"

"I'll be sleeping in the clinic. Come meet me."

When I walked down the hall to the clinic, I didn't know if she was going to come. I didn't know if I wanted her to come. Knight Ryder was on night duty at the clinic. I relieved him, told him I was meeting someone, and that he could go home. Ten minutes later, the sergeant opened the clinic door.

"Are you awake? I guess I do owe you one, but you better get your shit together; this is a one-time thing."

Chapter Six

The Godfather

The next day, I was still feeling bad when I reported to the hospital. I had many things running through my mind when the first patient came to my table. He was a short, chubby fellow with a face that made you want to laugh.

"Alright, buddy, what's going on?"

"Nothing, really. Back home I get my ears cleaned out every month or so, and it's just that time again."

"I'm sorry, you want me to clean your ears? You can't clean your own fucking ears? You know what, get the fuck out of my office. Get up and get out."

Before he could say anything else, I said, "Next patient, please."

Everyone was shocked. Still thinking she could remedy my attitude with reprimands Sgt. LT decided to write me up; a couple days of extra duty never hurt anyone. In fact, it made me feel like I was getting something done, and not to mention that the evenings were getting a lot more interesting.

VLA was becoming a living, breathing organization. It evolved from practical jokes and messing with the command to not giving a shit what the command thought and causing havoc throughout the base. We were getting an ample amount of alcohol from our families back home, and the women usually followed the alcohol. We laughed loudly and cursed out any neighbors who complained. People had the option to either join us or shut the fuck up. We drank on our days off, and we drank on our days on. We drank during mortar attacks, and we drank during power outages. We drank until we were out of liquor and couldn't hustle up anymore. We realized very quickly that our families were unreliable and that we needed a new supplier. When questions started being asked, answers came from an unlikely source.

Jagermiester: 25, 5'9" - VLA Status: Officer; would become Top Dog. Morals: Low. Jagermiester was an ex-marine who knew the field of communication to the T. He usually drank until he was belligerent, but that's why most of us loved him. He also enjoyed a good fight, which was always entertaining.

Jagermiester came to one of the rooms I had acquired to let me know that he found the land of milk and honey. His story was that on one of his communication flights, they had stopped in the Green Zone, Baghdad, for lunch. As most of the flight crew went to the dining facility, he and one of the crew chiefs decided to go to a little Chinese restaurant down the block. It was the same one that would later be suicide bombed. Here he saw a display cooler in the corner full of beer, imports, domestic, whatever. He told me that he asked to buy liquor from the man in charge, but he was deflected to a cook in the back. Here the cook sold him some Lebanon whiskey for a cheap price. The story put a smile on my face, but there were too many rumors going around for me to be too optimistic. I decided to check it out myself.

The next day that I had off, I set up a flight for me and three other VLA members who were off. Flights were easy to come by since my unit's mission was to fly high-priority personnel (Toby Keith, Conan O'Brien, John Stewart's people, you know high priority), and since they didn't come in too often, flights were usually open. Once we landed in Baghdad, we made our way to the restaurant. The story checked out, salty Chinese food, beer, even the disgusting kitchen that he described in great detail. I'm not saying that they were eating dogs, but the place did smell like dog shit; you figure it out. When I inquired into the sale, the cook sent me to a building behind the restaurant. Not knowing what to expect, I brought one man with me and left the other two at the restaurant for lookouts.

When we arrived at the back building, it appeared to be another restaurant, except this one was crawling with soldiers of strange crest, meaning units I didn't recognize. My copilot tried to bail, but I told him to sit down, enjoy some more Chinese food, and we'd scope the place out. The soldiers there looked as if they were on a sting operation. They were stalling, taking too long to eat, waiting for something. Finally, my copilot slapped me back into it.

"Look, I don't think I can eat any more fucking Chinese food. Either do this thing or we have to get out of here."

I began to laugh. He was right. We had to make a move before our bird arrived, our lookouts got tired, or someone got wise; it was just funny because he himself was of Asian descent. I called the twelve-year-old waiter over, and he pointed me to a door in the back. As I made my way back to the room, it felt like everyone had their eyes on me. When I opened the door, my focus went in every different direction. There were soldiers standing upright, four little Chinese men shucking corn, two Chinese women still lying in bed, and a pile of liquor so big it gave me a hard-on. As I looked back and forth at the soldiers, they became timid, like they were preparing to fight their way out of a corner. I smiled and winked at them.

"Carry on, men. I'm here for the same."

In fact, every soldier was there for the same, and every soldier there was as afraid of us as we were of them. I sat back down, and we waited our turn.

Once we returned to the landing zone, the bird was already there. As we loaded on, the pilots and the crew chiefs gave us a quick look over. With bags as full as ours, we were either smuggling whiskey or an Oompa Loompan sweat shop, that's right people, Willie Wonka's Chacolate factory was a fucking sweat shop. Well anyways, that night, to settle things over, I brought one of the crew chiefs four bottles as a payoff. One bottle for every ten brought back would become the usual air tax. It would be given to whomever we knew and trusted on the flight crew to be distributed to the rest of the personnel. Transportation and alcohol, check.

When it came to women, we needed help. Passing around the VLA *whores* was getting tiresome, not to mention that some of our guys started to get serious with them, and the Hawaiian unit wasn't expected for another month, so we decided to recruit someone from an outside unit.

Slim with the Tilted Brim: 19, 5'6" - VLA Status: Member. Morals: Low. Slim belonged to the Mississippi unit, yet no one was really sure what he did. For some reason, I don't think he owned a uniform, because he was always in civilian clothes. He had a thuggish demeanor, but he was harmless. Whatever his job was, it allowed him to travel across base every day.

Slim would make nightly trips to the other side of the base for the PX, or the theater, or Lord knows where, and he would spread the word of liquor and good times. Soon, he was approaching me daily to buy alcohol. Now he wasn't the most popular in his unit, so I figured he was drinking with guest. One night, Knight Ryder, Arilious, and I decided to relieve him of his female guest. He then realized that he was just a middle man, and once we had our own connection to the women, he'd be cut out completely. After that, he brought women to us. At least then he could drink, party, and hit on women without worrying about any of the three running out. Women, check.

As the men continued drinking, the black market liquor sales increased. Everyone and their roommates became distributors. There were no hard feeling over this, in fact quite the contrary; we revolved around each other. If one didn't have liquor, the other did. It's what made Mo-town the town square of Mortaritaville. Although VLA wasn't in a rush to appoint a leader, this job would be done by the barrage of consumers in and out of Mo-town. While the rest of the men became weary of selling liquor to anyone they didn't know and more importantly selling liquor until they didn't have enough for themselves, I gave liquor to those I didn't know until I didn't have a drop left. It would bring loyalty and a nickname: the *Godfather*. Although my men never called me the *Godfather*, and I didn't expect them to, the name would start to spread throughout the other units.

Everything was in place. The only thing left to do was monopolize.

Chapter Seven

The Scars Left on a Soldier's Journal

Soldiers of war can sometimes be described as separated from reality, some may even venture to say "off". Well, I've known a soldier whose wife used his sixteen thousand dollar reenlistment bonus on her student loans and left him while he was in Iraq. Another who's virgin girlfriend slept with another man while he was there. And still another whose toddler son was going through a crippling bone disease while he was there. These men had unthinkable problems, and if "off" is the way to describe them, then being "off" was being one tough son of a bitch. I, on the other hand, couldn't hold a candle to these guys. I had no such noteworthy problems and I rarely spoke of my family or the troubles I was having. Most of the men would probably say that I had a perfect life back home, and I had no reason to correct them. I felt that if I ever had a problem big enough to lay on someone else's shoulders it certainly wouldn't be any man going through harder times than me. As for the others, they usually wouldn't come to me, but every once in a while one would get lost and stumble through my door.

On one noteworthy evening Big Vin stopped by for a cordial and a heart to heart. Sadly, Big Vin lost his father in the same manner that we're losing some of our soldiers. Suicide shouldn't be considered dishonorable or weak, it's just the counteraction to the belief that the good that can come from ones continued living will never prevail over the evil and the pain caused by ones past. Any man is capable under the right circumstances, even the strongest. I'm not sure why Big Vin came to me, I didn't consider myself the best listener, and surely I wasn't the most sympathetic, but I gave him an ear... and a shoulder. We talked until early morning and Big Vin passed out in the middle of the floor.

The next morning I was awoken by Big Vin exiting the room, for a man his size he was actually quite graceful. No sooner had the door closed that I returned to dreaming of a Christmas morning backyard football game. In this particular dream it was the Christmas my father gave me the new *Nerf* Whistling football. A football that whistled as it flew through the air. I could even hear it getting tossed back and forth. I opened my eyes and sat up, my mind, I thought, was still recalling the sound. I continued to hear the cushioned football being thrown through the air, then finally the roar of explosion. Early morning mortar attacks weren't unusual, but hearing the mortar's fins whistle through the air was. I grabbed my rifle and lowered my shoulder to the door only to be slung back into the room by an unknown force. With a little more subtlety this time I opened the door about six inches and reached my hand out to see what was in the way... it was Big Vin.

"Get your ass to the bunkers Vin!" He didn't answer, I wasn't sure if he was injured or dead. I backed up again and took two hard steps into the half opened door. Pushed by the door, Big Vin slid to the right side of the steps. I lost my balance, missed every step and ended with my knees in the sand, rifle lost during the fall. Looking up at Big Vin, he didn't seem injured, just dazed. He was standing on the top step looking straight up. As my eyes followed the vertical line of his body into the air, I was speechless. Smoke trails, some still perfectly formed, some dissipating rapidly, but none were over ten feet above Big Vin's head. Crawling to my rifle the whistling began again, this time I witnessed myself the barrage of mortars following the same trail as the earlier ones. I quickly made it to my feet, grabbing Big Vin I started to the bunkers. Big Vin came to as I pushed him off the steps. When we rounded the corner I looked back to see where the mortars were landing. Most had landed on the airfield, some in the vacant "future site of the gym". Casualties should be at a minimum I thought. Then, just as I pushed Big Vin into the bunker, the whistling noise became deafening. This round was low, it would definitely drop into the soldiers living area.

The mortar's landing was like an explosion itself, sand was tossed into the air five feet, there was an echoing thump as it dug into hard ground. The mortar landed under a housing trailer in the next pod not but fifty yards away. Utilizing Cold War munitions, the Iraqi mortars only have a one in three chance of exploding. I cringed in waiting for the boom.

It's funny how your mind plays tricks during these situations. Details are blurry, timelines fade, and a journal is possibly a soldier's only form of memory. Sadly, on days like this my journal was left blank. The only reason I recall it now is because in the next day's entry I referred back to it with two sentences. "*Big Vin's ol' man killed himself, don't bring it up again. For future reference Big Vin froze up.*" I find that there are a lot of entries missing during these types of events. My journal never mentions any casualties even though I was there when an American tank ran over a British jeep killing three and again when the Dining Facility on the opposite side of base was mortared killing many. Thinking back on it now, I can't even remember if the jeep incident was day or night. The human brain is an amazing suppressor, and thankfully so. For this is one of the major reasons I omitted from this book the side of war that portrays human suffering.

After that day things became different. An unspoken change in demeanor occurred overnight. With the thought of death dropping out the sky the men lost their tolerance for the command's bullshit and naturally decided to declare me Top Dog. There's no doubt that this insubordination wouldn't come without a price, but we felt it was a means of survival. As the men were going through the toughest time in their lives, I believe the VLA helped take their minds off of it. In our minds we ran the show, maybe a false sense of accomplishment, but it was enough to get us through each day. The VLA became a sanctuary that couldn't be touched by the command, but just as soon as it couldn't be controlled it became a threat, and me leading it definitely didn't help out our standing with the command.

As I gave up all military etiquette, the men began to use the same habitual respective gestures to acknowledge me. When I decided that I wouldn't salute any longer the men began to salute me. They would stand with a half cocked smile when I entered the room. If they were ever questioned by any officer for wrong doing they would simply reply "It was LeJeune's orders, Sir." The men did it to show their malcontent for the command, but everyone insinuated that there was some sort of rank structure to our organization and I was in a position that demanded respect. Any man that was present would say that I demanded nothing, I simply did what I thought necessary to better the VLA, and the men followed, and with these men there were few places I wouldn't venture, even into the world of selling sex.

Catch and Release Program - A program put into place to distribute the few women stationed in war zones to the many men also there. The rules were simple. No male was allowed to date or to keep a female to himself exclusively for any period of time unless said male and female were together prior to deployment. Lastly, no male was to get upset when the redistribution phase came into effect.

I'm not sure what group of wise men put this ingenious plan into effect, but if I remember correctly the CRP was one of the rules passed down from war since the beginning of time. The idea most likely originated from the same men and during the same time period that Desert Ranking did, and it worked beautifully for the first half of our deployment. There were no female instigated fights, nor were there any men suffering from the lack of affection. Everyone was abiding to the laws and things were going smoothly, but given enough time any two people were bound to become attached. The laws bestowed on us by the forefathers of war were beginning to be ignored by everyone. Even officers in the VLA were beginning to use terms like "girlfriend" and "ol' lady". And like all empires throughout history, when order fails the first thing to expect is the oldest profession becoming the newest crave.

Rumors of female soldiers prostituting themselves were something to talk about, like the weather or last night's game. I never believed it nor felt the urge to seek out the truth. It was just something to make a few jokes about, make the night go by. Well, on this particular night it wasn't even on the back of anyone's mind. It was card night. Giff, Breezy, AA, a few of the other officers and myself sitting down to some *Spades*. If you're unaware of the game *Spades* get on any computer, go to its games, and look up *Hearts*, it's basically the same concept. Well, as the night went on I must have done exceptionally well, because I still had a couple of dollars in my pocket and I was participating in the last match. When I saw DH3 poke his head through the door I hadn't a clue he was there to bring the downfall of my faith in humanity.

"Doc, someone's out here to see you."

"Send him to Knightryder." I said without picking up my head.

"It's a her, Doc."

"Well in that case, what's the rule one?"

"Rule one? I forget."

"Never send women to Knightryder's room, it's like throwing meat to a fuckin' lion. I'll talk to her."

To my surprise it was a girl I had never met before. Not from my unit or any of the surrounding ones. I gave her a good look, the kind of look that can probably be mistaken for flirting. She was in little pink shorts and an Army grey and black sweatshirt. She was probably 5'4", good shape, and a face that was welcoming. The moment eye contact was made I went back to my cards.

"So what is it that I can do for you, hun?"

"A friend of mine said that I could buy some liquor from you."

"Sure you can, darling. How many bottles?"

"Fifteen."

"Fifteen!" I started to laugh, "I don't have that many here. Why don't you ask that guy that brought you here to take you to Knightryder's room. He'll be able to help."

As the woman exited, the game began again with the laughter at a minimum. I can't remember now if we won or lost but I do know that the room was empty when I received a faint knock at the door. Still gripping a whisky filled cut water bottle I answered it. The same little girl that went on a search for Knightryder found her way back.

"Did you find him, sweetheart?"

"Yeah, I found him. He told me to pay you."

"How much did he say that you owe me?" I was confused, usually Knightryder took the money.

"Well, I was hoping I could pay you in another form."

"Yeah, that's what you were hoping, huh? Well, I usually just take cash."

I've never seen a sweatshirt removed so fast. The girl was obviously a pro, grabbing the back of her neck with both hands and lifting her elbows into the air to make her breast look perky, staring me up and down slowly only to stop her eyes on my crotch. She knew how to work a guy. Sadly, she just wasn't my type.

"Put your shirt back on, please. Go to Knightryders room, I'm sure he'll take that form of currency. Then I'll get square with him.

Taking my seat on the bed I caught myself. "Actually, go to any door in Mo-town, someone will pay me back."

"Really, all of you like to party?"

"Party? These guys are fuckin' animals. They'll eat you alive, sweetheart."

"Well, tell all of your boys that me and some of my girlfriends are always open for business."   "Business?" I said like a confused little boy. "You're with the hookers from across base?"

"We're not hookers, we just like to party. And if your guys want to party with me its five hundred dollars per person."

"Honey, where I'm from we call that hooking, and those who do it are hookers."

"Whatever," says the hooker. "Are we going to do this or do you want cash?"

"The liquors free if I can take a look at your log book. The names of all the Johns that you've serviced."

"A log book. Are you serious?"

"What," I said laughingly. "Is a hooker with superb record keeping skills too much to ask for these days?"

"You know what; I'll just give you cash."

Never wanting to miss a black market opportunity I replied, "How about a commission? I'll supply you with alcohol and new clientele, and you pay me a percentage of your nightly wages."

With a look of disgust, that's right a hooker gave me a look of disgust, she threw the cash on the bed and showed herself out. A few weeks later I ran into someone who apparently was a mutual friend of both of ours. He asked if I really tried to become her pimp. After hours of arguing and with all of my points exhausted I realized that I did. Without even knowing it I tried to become the men I think the least of.

Although I truly believe that everyone is a whore to the money, not everyone is the pimp. Selling yourself, whether it be your keen intellect, your strong back, or your body; is just a part of a good man's life. A pimp, on the other hand, is the user, just an exploiter of others, the proverbial man. Looking back on it, I realize that as many hours as I put in trying to ruin the man, I became him.

Once I realized the path that led me here I began to realize how our politicians become what they are. They start their career on the basis that someone before him has fucked over the people and that he's there to help. Then 5, 10, 20 years pass and he ends his career by fucking over the people. I was on this path, it was the path of self-destruction.

Chapter Eight

Hello, Moto

Long nights and hard days continued for a couple more weeks until we were hit with a godsend. The Hawaiian unit's arrival was anticipated by everyone. Our imaginations ran wild with women, ukuleles, and luaus, and on this particular day, the only thing between us and them was about three hundred miles of hostile territory. For selfish reasons, we all were praying for them to make it safely, and safely they made it.

While some of the boys and I were out sun tanning, a convoy of Humvees turned the corner into our territory. Now it wasn't odd to us, four males getting down to our brown *draws*, putting some white shit on our noses, and sitting in the sun drinking highballs, but they must have thought we were nuts. The group of us were silent, watching beautiful woman after beautiful woman jump down from those big, mean deuce-and-a-halfs; it was like seeing a hot girl driving a big truck. Those little brown *draws* couldn't hold back my excitement. We were in awe, or shock and awe. I'm not sure who broke the silence, but it didn't break our concentration.

"That must be the..."

"Shut up."

"They were supposed to be..."

"We know."

It was a sight to be taken in. Beautiful women trying to shake sand out of places that I can't mention here, surfer dudes who kind of brought a little bit of Hawaii with them. I needed to be in that mix. I decided to wait a day to let them settle in, wind down from the convoy.

The next day, after collecting some bottles from one of the men who flew to the Green Zone that day, I took a stroll to their pod area. What I was looking for was a young man who was breaking

Army rules in a subtle, harmless way. What I found was a young man with an anarchy sticker on his door just above an upside down American flag (which means distress). His boots weren't bloused and his sleeves were rolled once, which isn't in any uniform standard that I've ever heard of. This was my guy; he was the one who could get my foot in the door.

"How's everything? Ya'll getting settled in well?"

"What's up, name's Moto."

Moto: 19, 6'1" - VLA Status: Hawaiian Officer. Morals: Medium Low. Moto was a young buck and a borderline anarchist. He hated Bush, command, and anything else in charge. He was intelligent, ambitious, or goal oriented, and he became a friend. He wasn't the most famous in his unit, but with my help, he did become the most infamous.

"Well, Moto, think of me like a liaison. I can get whatever you need...with a small price."

Directly behind me, sitting on the opposite steps was a haole, pronounced howly (white man to the Hawaiians) who spoke up.

"You know where to gamble?"

"There's a poker game every Tuesday in pod area 9. I'm sorry, what's your name?"

"Dave"

Dave: 30ish, 6'3" - VLA Status: (H) Officer. Morals: Low. Dave and Moto were inseparable. They hated each other one day and loved each other the next. Dave even swung on young Moto one night. He was smart and did his job to stay under the radar but, like me, he loved to drink.

"Can you find liquor?" Moto spoke up.

"Find it? I'll tell you what, here's two bottles on the house. Welcome to Mortaritaville. If you need anything else, I'll be back tomorrow."

With that, I declared my new territory and walked away with a smile. Little did I know that the Hawaiians had no intentions of letting me get out of their world unscathed. Before it was over, there was more liquor, women, weed, smuggling, sex, and violence than I could handle, but it was sure fun getting to that last straw.

I began to separate my time between Mo-town and Surf-city. That being said, I began to converse less and less with the VLA and felt a little like I was betraying them in some way. They had made me who I had become, and I turned my back as soon as I found something better. Of course, they let me come and go as I pleased, always with a warm welcome. They just treated my relationship with the Hawaiians like it was business, but deep down I knew I enjoyed the company of the Hawaiians more than my guys in Mo-town. I think it was something about their laid-back ways, or how they just laid around, or maybe I was just trying to get laid. Nonetheless, everyone was trying to keep the peace except for me.

One drunken night, I strolled into Mo-town and began to converse with one of the VLA officer's girlfriends. This was the kind of girl who had tattoo sleeves and turned wrenches for a living . One thing led to another, and the whiskey took over. When I finished, it was morning.

"I'm going to run. I suggest you be gone by the time I get back."

When I returned, she was gone, and it wasn't till that evening that I realized that it wasn't a game to everyone else as it was to me. People were hurt, and bonds were broken. Across the walk, I could hear DH3 screaming at his girlfriend with a crowd waiting outside his door.

"Get the fuck away from me. Go to his room if you want to cry."

Sob, sob, sob.

"I know you been wantin' to fuck him; now you did. Congratulations."

Sob, sob, sob.

Then I heard the voices get louder, indicating that the door to his room was open now. I opened my door just to make sure he didn't hit her. He grabbed her by the arm and slung her down the steps. He and I looked at each other for a second. As I ate my canned pears, he finally said what I was hoping he'd say.

"It's not your fault. She's a whore. I'm not mad at you. You have any more of those pears?"

I threw him a can, closed my door, and walked back in my room. I had no control over myself or what I did. I was the worst kind of loose cannon, one that wasn't loose at all, one that intentionally fired on friendly forces. I was so delusional that I was more upset with her for telling him than I was at myself for letting it happen.

Thinking back on it now makes me sad, but then I can't say I felt any remorse.

Kenny, I'm sorry about the following if you didn't already know.

Kenny and Wife: 20, & 20; 5'8" & 5'5" - VLA Status: Officer, Member. Morals: Medium Low & Low. They married young to reap the benefits of a marriage in the military, simultaneous deployment, shared living quarters and so on. They both loved their marijuana and, other than that, they had nothing in common. Kenny was a cool, laid-back cat, and the wife was a loud drama queen, but even the most obnoxious women can get attention when they look like her.

Kenny's wife and I began a relationship also. What can I say? When you're on a roll, why not destroy everyone who loves you? We began to find each other in the shadows of parties. Although we never surpassed kissing, the situation came to the breaking point, and no one even knows until now.

One night, the wife came to one of the rooms that she knew I was in while I was asleep. She woke me up to give me more information than any man should get when still half asleep.

"I'm divorcing Kenny, and I'm moving in here with you."

"What?"

"I'm going to Topp tomorrow to see if me and Kenny could separate. Then I could move in here."

"Seriously, are you nuts? Where is Kenny now?"

"He's at work." Saying while she pushed me aside to sit down.

"You have to get out of here."

Right then I heard the loudest bang on the door I've ever heard.

"Oh my God, that's him."

"Thanks for the update, honey. Does he have his gun?" Trying to pull my covers from under her ass now.

"I don't know"

Then came a rapid knock on the window and a muffled voice: "Hey, go'dammit, he's coming." It was DH3 letting us know that Kenny was on his way back from work and joining the party that was going on outside my door. I quickly jumped up, grabbed her by the arm, and pushed her out of my door. I grabbed my gun and jumped back in my bed. When I heard Kenny and Knight

Ryder walk up and begin talking, I knew we were in the clear. A few moments later, I opened the door and told DH3 to come and see me over all the voices calling me a pussy and a weak drinker.

"How did you know she was in here?"

"Everyone knows, buddy."

"What does that mean?"

"We've known for weeks. We see her sneaking in here every night. Don't worry, no one's going to tell Kenny. You know, buddy, you fuck my girlfriend, you fuck his wife..."

"We never fucked."

"I don't care, buddy."

"Alright get out, and hey, I owe you and the guys one for this."

"I know, buddy."

Jealous husbands are dangerous enough, but one that has to carry a weapon at all times gives me the shakes. I was on the fence between being in a mafia movie and being the end of one. Sadly, I had to rely on a man I had screwed over, and thank the Lord he was much more loyal than I was.

The wife and I continued the relationship until she left. Not surprisingly, she was more trouble than I first anticipated. By the end, she had told a room full of people that we had slept together, started two other relationships, and screwed another one of the VLA officers. Kenny was way too good for her, and I hope he's come to realize it now. Kenny, I'll completely understand if you decide to kill me, but I just wanted to let you know...kill Knight Ryder first.

The next day, I sent Slim with the Tilted Brim to find a woman for DH3 as a condolence for what I had done and a thanks for what he had done. When I had gone to tell DH3 to expect company, he had already picked up a new dame. She looked like an ugly man with Down syndrome, but he was content. A man with no standards doesn't need help finding a woman. If you've ever seen *Crybaby* with Johnny Depp, Hatchet Face should come to mind, but he wasn't the only one dipping his doodle in that. On a few occasions, I caught Big Vin dancing with the devil. Apparently, she had something special, and I was missing out. If you had seen her back in the U.S., you would literally walk to the other side of the street. Alright, I'm done knocking on this poor girl. Big Vin, DH3, you both are sick sons of bitches. Sorry, mama Heintz.

The girls Slim brought back for DH3 were now mine. I decided to go and retrieve Knight Ryder and get the party started. The girls who stood before us when we opened the door would become legendary in the VLA.

The Scallywags: VLA Status: *Whores*. The scallywags were Active Army girls from, I think, the Big Red One unit. They thought that their own active duty personnel were too strict and enjoyed getting away to Mo-town. They loved sex and were bisexual after the consumption of enough drinks. They ranged from two to four women most nights.

Four petite women (two blondes, a strawberry blonde, and a brunette), all corrupted by the Army way of life. They drank, cursed, danced, screwed, and videotaped all of it. Knight Ryder and I quickly picked up on the two cutest ones, and they were back in our rooms before we could find condoms.

The girl with me explained that, throughout her five-year relationship with her boyfriend, she had never had an orgasm. This didn't discourage me one bit.

With a huge smile on my face, I said, "Well, let me give it a try."

I brought my A game. I sweated for hour after hour until sunrise to no avail. Finally, when she rolled over from on top of me she smashed my self-esteem.

"I told you so!"

Quickly, I answered back, "You're right, and it's kind of an ego bust, so get the fuck out."

"Why are you mad? I mean, I like you."

"Thanks, get your shit."

At that time, my door opened and it was Knight Ryder's scallywag. I need to learn to lock my door.

"Knight Ryder said you need to get to work."

"Is Knight Ryder my keeper?"

"I guess not," she said, jumping in bed with us.

"So, what did you two do last night? And can you do it again this morning?"

My scallywag spoke up. "We just finished." She threw her arm around me like we'd been lovers for ten years.

"Oh, my God. Did you really?" the scallywag asked, putting her hand on my chest.

Here's the dilemma. I really should have been at the hospital. I had two girls in bed, one of which I couldn't satisfy the night prior and the other willing to give me a helping hand. I had had no sleep, and my last sip of whiskey was five minutes ago.

"Alright, let's give it a try."

The last thing I remember was trying to get one of their bras off. The next thing I knew I was waking up to a knock on the door. Neither of the girls was there anymore. I never bothered getting dressed to open the door, but I probably should have thought about it this time. It was Sgt. LT.

"Why aren't you at work?"

"I'm taking off."

"No, you are not; get dressed and report to the hospital."

"Hold your breath."

"You know what, I'm not even arguing with you. Your papers came in today for your two weeks R&R vacation. I'm sending them back; you're not going anywhere."

"Wait, when?"

"You were supposed to leave in two weeks, but..."

"Sgt. LT., listen. I'm getting dressed. I'll be there in ten minutes. Don't do anything drastic. I was just joking. I'm coming."

R&R, two weeks in the States to wind down. I might not have been soldiering very hard, but I damn sure needed a vacation, away from husbands with guns, officers with egos, and women with future aspirations. I was Sgt. LT.'s bitch for the next two weeks, and she knew it. I wouldn't even sigh in her direction. I was once again a soldier, or at least I held the image of a soldier.

On the day before I left, I took orders from the men for their preference of domestic alcohol, porn, or whatnot. That night, to celebrate, a couple of guys and I sat down to drink the only Everclear that was ever obtained out there and we even aquired some steak from the DFAC. We had fun, discussing the first thing I was going to do when I got home, food I was going to eat, and things I was going to take time to enjoy, like rain. I notified the men that I was going to sleep and to make sure that I was awake in time to catch my bus. Now, I'm not sure what happened after that, but the next morning, they found me outside of my room in a lawn chair with the bottle of Everclear still in hand. From what I understand, they had to dress me and pack my shit. When I came to, Knight Ryder was standing over me saying, "I thought you were dead."

"Not dead, just drunk."

"No, I put an IV in each arm and I forgot to fill the tube. I just pumped a whole tube of air into your veins," he said, giggling.

"Jesus, that's enough to give me a heart embolism."

"Sorry."

Sorry for almost killing me. I don't think sorry was enough, but I couldn't stay mad at something that cute. Hell, I was probably dreaming about him before he woke me. With that I made it to my feet. When I looked around, there must have been fifteen people in my room just to make sure I made it. They were good men...except for one thing. As a joke, they had put my helmet on backwards, and I never noticed. In fact, I made it all the way to the plane like that. Never mind, not good men, they were assholes.

On the walk to the bus, The Lieutenant joined me. Apparently, they decided to send me with an escort.

"Here's your orders. Shut the fuck up, and don't start any shit. You're not my problem once we get to the States."

"An escort, I feel special. And one so big and manly."

Upon entering the bus, I noticed a large, scared-faced sergeant. I made sure to sit behind him.

"Hey. Buddy."

"What?"

"I have a bad feeling we're not going to make it through the flight. Well, actually...just you."

"What is your problem, asshole?" he said, after an intimidating stare.

The lieutenant turned around and used his best officer voice. "Shut the fuck up, sorry sergeant; pay no attention to him."

"Turn around and catch your breath, lieutenant." I winked at the sergeant in front of me.

We finally made it to the plane without killing each other. It was a long flight, but surprisingly, the officers did their best to ease the tension. Halfway through the flight, one of the junior officers had an idea. He collected most of the officers on the flight, put them all in flight attendant coats, and began to serve meals. Immediately, our minds were sprung out of Iraq. Officers were humanized and taking an extra step to show it. These men got in drag to put a smile on the lower enlisted faces. It is one thing I never forget when other soldiers start to bash officers. To whoever that officer was who conducted that, you are the true soldier, just a man who sometimes has to carry a gun. Thank you.

Chapter Nine

This Isn't the Home I Left

Upon our arrival at the airport, there was a warm welcome from the civilian sector. It made us feel loved even though I knew that personally I deserved none of it. But that warm feeling would be interrupted by a gut-wrenching one.

"Did you boys know that they had the elections?"

"I'm not from Texas, sir."

"No, the elections in Iraq."

The elections weren't scheduled for a couple of weeks, but the powers that be decided to do the ol' Kansas City Shuffle. It felt like we had abandoned our men at one of the most detrimental and possibly deadliest points of our tour, but it was a relief to hear that the plan worked and minimum casualties were taken. That feeling of worry and panic would never subside through my vacation.

The world didn't stop because we went to war, and the war didn't stop when we got home. There is a constant fear of returning to both worlds. The man that people at home knew didn't exist anymore. Although this book does not depict the bad sides of the war, I'm sure that the people are smart enough to figure it out. Even the depiction that this book does give changes men in unthinkable ways. We are animals in either aspect of the war, and to return home and be civilized on cue is much harder than one would think. We're forced to portray two different personalities, both of which are diluted by what the two worlds think we should be. We overcompensate to be normal in both worlds, until we have no real self anymore. Until we are what you want us to be, in a state of constant disguise, not only in words, but in actions and personality. In this state is how my family saw me for the first time.

Now I'm not going to get into the whole reunion and family humbug, but I will say that my brother and one of my sisters had gotten married. My mother was suffering from severe anxiety because of my absence. My father was still as tough as nails and awaited my full return. My youngest sister, who holds my heart, was doing fine trying to find her path in life, and believe it or not, Hollie and I reunited.

Give me a break, we were together for five years...but I guess that's not all. She reminded me of who I was before all this bullshit, the real me. Forgiveness, I thought, came easy because of all that I had done. If we just wiped the slate clean, then we would make it alright. I couldn't picture my future without her. Till this day, I have met no woman like her. I knew she'd make a great mother and wife. I knew that under her training, my children would make up for all of my mistakes, that she would keep me in line when my head became too big and, most of all, she loved unconditionally. Another thing was that she cried when we first saw each other, and I used to tell her that "crying never solved any problems." I used to tell her that so that her crying didn't bring tears out of my eyes. I wanted her to be strong like I wasn't. I wanted her to be everything that I wasn't. I think that's what got to me the most when she fell to lust, that she was just as weak as I. I couldn't help but fall immediately back in love with her when I saw her eyes water up, no matter what she had done.

After a trying two weeks at home, I found myself back at the airport in Texas, sharing stories with some guys from my unit and drinking them away at the same time. I can't say that I didn't want to get back, back to my men and away from all of this complicated shit. As civilian patriots continued to pay for our food and our drinks, I began to tie one on. Just about the time I became loud and unruly, The Lieutenant found me.

"Alright, you're with me again."

"Lieutenant, so glad you could make it. I see you didn't waste your time on salads this past two weeks."

"The plane's leaving in an hour; there's a bar right onside of the terminal; you can drink there."

I followed The Lieutenant to the bar, where I found a young dame waiting to ship off to Navy or Air Force boot camp. I sparked up a conversation with her, and the next thing I knew we were in the airport restroom. This might sound like bullshit, but The Lieutenant knows it to be true. Later, he would say that he thought she was a he, but with the eyes I had on, she could have been a George Foreman grill and I would have screwed it. I was back, once again the man who all of my men expected me to be. When I was finished, I found The Lieutenant waiting for me in the same seat as before.

"You're cut off!"

"C'mon, Lieutenant, one more drink."

"No, no more drinks!"

"Alright, you're right." Addressing the barkeep now, I said, "Ma'am, one more drink for me and my fat friend please."

With that, The Lieutenant stood up and shuffled away, leaving me and my new friend to say good-bye.

The flight back was long, and I was as drugged up as Willie Nelson, but when we finally arrived, night had already fallen on Mortaritaville, and I prepared to sleep off the rest of my sleeping pills. My slumber and dreams of being Jack Sparrow came to an abrupt end at 0300 (3:00 a.m.) in the morning.

Chapter Ten

If I'm Not Back in Five, Send the DART Team

One of the DART team leaders stood out of breath at my front door.

"Are you drunk?"

"No, Vic. what's wrong?"

"A Chinook just went down outside of a small village north of Baghdad. They activated the DART team. We're on in thirty; be on the flight line in ten."

Now this is how a war is supposed to work, people out of breath, talking in lingo that even I didn't understand, panic, fear, and excitement all wrapped into the same stupid facial expression. I threw on my armor and was on the flight line in five. As I walked up, the team smiled, not because it was good to see me, but they knew Priest had been on R&R with me, and if I was back, then he was back.

Priest: 20, 5'3" - VLA Status: Member. Morals: High. Priest was a tiny Filipino who was an integral part of the DART team. Since the team was made up of the craziest SOBs in the unit, we figured God didn't care for us much. On the other hand, Priest was one of the most humble, God-fearing men that I had ever met. Therefore, with him on the crew, we figured God would have a harder time disposing of us.

The problem was that Priest had been held up in Kuwait and hadn't made it back with me. The guys were a little on edge. Sgt. Maj. began handing out grenades and RPGs like they were candy and he was on *To Catch a Predator*. The men were cocked, locked, and ready to rock.

During our briefing, it was good to see one of the best pilots we had coming with us, but onside of him was a lanky pilot that no one had ever seen before. He had a look on his face like we were about to hit Normandy beach on mopeds.

"Alright, load the birds, men, and be safe."

Because the medic is always the last one out of the bird, I was the first to load. In front of me was the mysterious guest pilot, loading into the seat opposite me. When he turned around, I could tell he was spooked.

"Have you all ever done this before?" He said with trouble.

"Nope, should be fun."

"Really? No, you're joking. I'm the replacement Chinook pilot; ya'll gotta keep me safe."

With a shit-eating grin to reassure him, I yelled to the back of the line. "Jagermiester, pick up the go'damn morale."

Jagermiester was famous for his tension-breaking song, Bonnie Tyler's "Total Eclipse of the Heart." Every time before a mission, or before the shit got thick, he would break into it.

"I fucking need you more tonight, I fucking need you more than ever, and if you'd only hold me tight, we'd be holding on forever."

Or something like that, but it would always make the men smile. This particular time might have been inappropriate since the pilot with us was scared shitless. The funny thing was that, during the flight, DH3's face became similar. Every man on the team watched fear sneak down his *draws* and grab him by the nuts. We were all a little shook up, but we all did our best to make our jokes and laugh even if they weren't funny.

"Ay, Doc, if I get killed, I want you to change my will and leave everything to a girl I just met on the Internet named Hollie."

"Oh yeah, you think she's the one?"

"I don't know, she's got a boyfriend out here, but if he don't make it, I'll sure as hell give it a try. In fact, I just heard the pilot say that there's too much weight on the bird and that you should jump out."

Everyone laughed except for the Chinook pilot and DH3. Then the call came back. "LZ in three!"

The bird set down in a garden outside of a small village. The perimeter was covered on the village side by a ground unit that apparently came from Baghdad. The Chinook was immediately entered by a team of mechanics and our Chinook pilot. As they worked, our team was dispersed on the south side of a farm. They all took their fields of fire and waited. I decided to make my rounds and check on the guys shortly thereafter. When I came upon Jagermiester, he was staring at what looked like a ripped garbage bag of hay lying in the ditch about fifty yards in front of him.

"What you got, Jagermiester?"

"I thought it was something, but it just looks like hay."

"You sure?"

"Yeah."

"Alright, be quite; I'm gonna go mess with DH3."

By the time I made it to DH3, he was in high spirits that we had ground forces to back us up.

"DH3, how's it going?"

"Hey, buddy."

"Holy shit, DH3, what's in that ditch? It looks like a sniper."

"What is that?" he said, quickly turning his rifle to the bag of hay.

"I don't know, sir, but it was good knowing you."

Then I got to my knees and snapped one of my proudest salutes. If it were a sniper, as DH3 thought it was, he would have recognized my salute as an indication that DH3 was an officer, which he wasn't, and would have immediately gone for a kill shot. Although dangerous, it was fun to watch DH3 squirm.

"Doc, Doc, you son of a bitch. I can't believe you would do that." His voice got louder as I moved to the next person.

All the men got a good chuckle, but no one was hurt, and all equipment and personnel made it back safely.

Upon our return, we were debriefed and then told that today was our last DART mission and our active-duty component was going to take over from this point forward. It wasn't a shock, hell, they took away everything else, but it was a little depressing. After that, it became a joke.

"I'm going to the pisser. If I'm not back in five minutes, activate the DART team."

Chapter Eleven

Let Me Live in the Pharmacy, I'll Be Good

When I finally arrived at my room later that day, I was visited with good news. Knight Ryder came to let me know that Sgt. LT. had left on her R&R and that we'd be rid of her for two weeks. To top it off, the pharmacy, which was equipped with a bedroom, had just become vacant of Mic G, who was working as our pharmacy tech, and was available for me. Apparently, Mic G decided to get back into the battalion living area to be closer to the good times and women. The guys and I went immediately into moving mode, and I was set up before midnight, another quaint little place to call home.

The pharmacy was perfect for every reason. First of all, it was miles away from the battalion living area and anything resembling command. Second, it was dark and damp, the perfect place to build a wine still. Third, it was ten feet away from the hospital for quick access to condoms, IVs, and a phone that reached the States (not that I ever used it). It was the perfect place to start a black glove operation, which means that there were too many people with the key to the pharmacy to pin a crime on any one. Another plus was that I could yell out of the door and schedule a flight to the Green Zone. It was perfect; hell, if I could, I'd raise my family there.

The second night I was in the room, Wild Bill came to update me on the new trend. He whipped out a bag of marijuana about the size of a nickel and told me, "This shit is going to take over the market."

Now, I prided myself on being able to say that I'd never put that shit to my lips once, especially where I come from, but staying on top of the game was also my business. So I decided what the hell. I have never laughed so much in my life; in fact, I was watching

American Beauty and my gut hurt. Now, there's no doubt that I enjoyed it myself, but one of my best friends from childhood became wrapped up in this game. I watched as that little plant planted him more times than he'd like to admit. I despised it and told Wild Bill that there was a difference between selling something that was legal in the States and selling something that wasn't. The risk was too high, and the profit was marginal. Also a plant that doesn't grow in abundance in Iraq would only entice the command to start searching mail, which would screw our man in sex toys, us in wine yeast, and completely infringe on our privacy. There was no need to get into it, especially now that the alcohol business was treating us so good. Now, I'm not claiming to be an angel because I did tell him to continue the market, but only for the men, not to push it through the base.

The pharmacy began to be the place for most of the black market dealings within the first week I was in there. There was a fifteen-day wait on wine, immediate pick-up on liquor, and a maybe, maybe not, on weed for the boys. The women could sneak off to the pharmacy, and no one would be the wiser. It became a vault of ecstasy, self-debauchery, and drunken stupidity. Think of it like the Neverland Ranch for soldiers; no, don't think of it like that, more like Amsterdam. The word spread, and it spread quickly.

One night while I was visiting my Hawaiian crew, I had one too many to drink. Later, I was told that I tried to fight two men who were already fighting each other, told two Hawaiian women that one wasn't good enough and I needed both of them, and passed out in the same place where everyone pissed. It must have been a hell of a night. When I came to, two Hawaiian men were carrying me to the pharmacy. As I opened my eyes, I noticed it was the same two guys who were trying to fight each other. By the time we had gotten to the pharmacy, I thought that they earned two bottles of whiskey on the house. I handed it over, and they were on their way. A few moments later, while I was lying in the bed, I heard the door open, then close. I knew right away that these two didn't realize who I was and were attempting to pillage some liquor. When I made it to the door, they were already about twenty feet away. All I had to do was whistle and point back into the room.

"What?" Attempting to act innocent.

"I'm not going to blame you two for something I would probably do when I'm drunk."

"What?"

I rubbed my forehead to show my aggravation.

"I thought you gave these to us. Sorry."

As they replaced the bottles that they had taken, they almost put back the bottles that I had given them.

"No, those are yours."

With that they thanked me and left.

One of the two men apologized to Moto and me for what he had done. We became good friends later in the tour and almost partners. The other continued not to like me but learned to respect me. On a few occasions, I found myself in his room over a few highballs. Truth is he was a lot like me, constantly trying to be hard, but really he was just a fun-loving SOB.

As the next couple of days passed, and Dave and Moto recapped that night's events, I learned that there was another player involved. He was a cop in the Hawaiian islands. Now, usually a cop and a criminal don't get along, but it was to my benefit to keep him happy. He respected what I did, and I respected him. The truth is, he was the only guy, American or Iraqi, that I feared. He was one of those chivalrous do-gooders who couldn't be bought by my bullshit or turned by instant satisfaction. It was probably transparent that I was afraid of him because, every time I was in town, I either sent someone with a bottle or delivered one to him myself. I think he also reminded me of my father, old school, quite enough not to be fucked with. You know the type. Alright, enough of kissing his ass.

As a footnote, I know that there was an investigation over eight hundred missing Valium from the pharmacy, but they had gone missing long after I had moved out. That's just for any inquiring minds.

It seems it was the same messenger of good news that brought the bad news. Knight Ryder woke me up with the news that Sgt. LT. was back, and she wasn't happy about what was going on in the pharmacy. The moment she arrived, she told me to move back to the battalion living area. Apparently, it wasn't all her decision. Almost every room that I had owned before was taken from me on that same day. That would be three rooms and a pharmacy that

I had to clear out of that day. The keys were to be turned in that evening. I didn't have to look for a snitch; I mean, I wasn't exactly trying to keep it out of the public eye. I'm pretty sure it was my loud mouth that brought the downfall of my safe houses. It made for a lot of liquor to relocate.

This was one event that foreshadowed a major command movement. They apparently were getting tired of my antics and boasting. They thought they had given me enough chances, and in return, I had just thrown it back in their faces, that they, not me, were the good guys, and it only took them seven months to realize that. In truth, the only one I felt sorry for was Topp. He was just trying to get to retirement and not make any waves. He wanted to make everyone happy, and controlling me would make everyone except me happy. It was a good plan, but I think he underestimated how far gone I was. At this point, it would take a lot more than, "Come on, Doc, help me help you."

I was relocated back with my first roommate, Fitz Gerald, with whom nothing but problems would arise. He complained about my hygiene. I'll admit I smelled of constant alcohol and sex, not to mention my sheets. I had a problem with his thirty piss bottles lying all over the floor. Our ways of living was the least of our problems. He thought I cared only for myself and used everyone to my advantage, and I thought he would do anything to get ahead in this man's Army, including selling his own friends to the command. I guess we both were right.

I hated being in the same room with him and spent most of my time with the Hawaiians. I also began drinking heavily every night. The only time I would enter the room was when it was time to pass out or to piss off the altar boy. It really was an unhealthy relationship, but I couldn't help making it worse. One night, I had a date with who I think was one of the Hawaiian girls. I couldn't find my backpack, so I took his to transport liquor in. The next morning, when I returned to the room, I threw his backpack inside and told him that there was a present inside for him. While I was at work, he decided to open up the bag to check what all the fuss was about. Can you imagine a kid going downstairs on Christmas morning, ripping at a present, looking up at daddy with a huge smile on his face, only to find...a used condom? Before I came home from the hospital, he had time to work up quite a fury.

When I opened the door, he was yelling at the top of his lungs. I laughed at him; we had only become too comfortable living alone because of my actions, because I moved out. I gave him privacy, I gave him personal time, and I gave him a used condom. He should've been thanking me. I blame it on myself. We couldn't do anything about each other, at least for another week.

Chapter Twelve

If I Could Stop Drinking, Then I'd
Just Be Insane

Masturbation was a healthy ritual in Iraq. Out there it was nothing to be ashamed of; it was constantly talked about, laughed about, and done in the open. When I moved back in with Fitz Gerald, I discovered he had boodles of porn, boxes of porn, porn under his mattress, porn in his locker, treasure maps that led him to hidden porn. Sometimes, I came home and found little pink post-its with romantic messages leading him to porn. Well, the room did offer more privacy than the showers, and to tell you the truth, I think Bell was conducting some sort of secret filming or internet site thing, I don't know. So I decided to conduct my self-defiling in the privacy of my own room while I was on Fitz Gerald's bed. I'm not sure why I had to do it on Fitz Gerald's bed. I mean, I could have turned the television to face my bed, but it was his TV, and I was trying hard to respect his stuff. Well, an unlocked door and five minutes later would lead to Fitz Gerald walking in and witnessing the holy union. I don't think I missed a beat, but with a mouth like his, the story could get worse. Before it was all over, I might have had a finger in my ass and a garbage bag over my head. So I decided to go to headquarters and tell everyone that I walked by what had happened. As everyone got a good laugh, I took a little bit of thunder away from Fitz Gerald.

By the time I made it to Topp and began telling him the story, I noticed two boxes and a couple of letters. With all the tomfoolery going on, I had forgotten to check my mail in a couple of weeks. I quickly made my way back to the room to read my mail and to find out what the boxes contained. The letters were from loved ones, and the boxes contained Crown Royal, my preferred drink at home. We couldn't find Crown out there, so it was a welcomed surprise. I decided to pull out some old letters and open the bottle of Crown. That bottle of Crown would begin what is known as my brain-cell genocide.

That night, after rereading most of the letters that I had collected and finishing the bottle of Crown, I decided to write Hollie an e-mail. I left my room and walked to Wild Bill's room to use his connection. I passed two or three parties but didn't stop. I could hear people screaming at me, but I was on a mission. When I opened Wild Bill's door, he was already using his computer as a radio for a small get-together he was having.

"Billy, when you're done, I'd like borrow your computer so I can write Hollie."

"Sure, cousin, but don't you think you should put some clothes on first?"

And there it was, that's why people were screaming at me and taking pictures, I was stark ass naked. When I looked down, the only article of clothing I had was a pair of Hollie's panties that she had sent me, and they were balled up in my hand.

"Thanks, Billy, come and get me when you're done."

While I walked back to the room, I felt like I was famous, with people whooping and hollering and flashes from cameras. This one wasn't going to make it under the radar. When I returned to my room, it didn't take twenty minutes for a recognizable voice to be heard over the crowd. It was The Lieutenant.

"Where's Doc?"

Then I heard Big Vin's voice. "I think he's in his room."

"Which one?"

"His old one."

The door opened, and I saw Big Vin's face.

"Doc, The Lieutenant wants to see you."

"Why?"

"Well, he wants to know if you know anything about someone walking around naked."

As I stepped onto the steps, I looked down at Big Vin.

"I don't know anything about that, but I do know this."

Then I leaned down and kissed Big Vin right on his fat lips, hands on both sides his face like the kiss that started a million marriages. It was magic. Apparently, he didn't enjoy it as much as

I. With one quick push, that big bastard knocked me off my feet, five feet away from my steps and flat on my back. I was hurt all over, and I couldn't get back up, but Big Vin's kind heart wouldn't let it go down like that. He walked over, calmly picked me up like a little baby, and put me in the bed.

"I'm sorry, buddy, I had to. You're just too drunk."

I loved that big guy. I still love that big son of a bitch.

That next evening, most of the VLA officers and members were all called into a meeting with the acting first sergeant.

Sgt. Joe: 40ish, 6'2" - VLA Status: Neutral. Morals: Medium Low. Sgt. Joe lived on cigarettes and coffee; hence, the name Joe. He made himself a necessity to the unit by being able to wheel and deal with other units. He knew how to get what he wanted and somehow always made it look like it would benefit the unit. Seriously, did we really need a cold war antiaircraft missile launcher? He was what I wanted to be if I hadn't had a soul.

Sgt. Joe decided that, instead of blaming the events of the night before on anybody, he would let us do the blaming. It was ingenious. All he asked was, "Who's the problem?" And wouldn't you know it, Fitz Gerald had something to say. The overgrown altar boy pointed directly at me. I wouldn't have been surprised to learn that he and Sgt. Joe had planned this shit out beforehand.

"Well, Doc, since I don't believe you have any more rank to take away, and you obviously don't give a shit about the small amount of money the Army pays you, I have a new idea," he said with that smile on his face. "But before I tell you the plan, I would first like to apologized for having to do it, also Topp, along with the rest of the command, has recognized Louisiana Saturday Nights in Mo-town, and"... Before he could say another word, all the guys began to yell and high-five. The room turned lively before my death sentence was sent down. He laughed and continued "they recognize your parties and, because it hadn't affected anything, there was no problem, but it has gotten too big, and it was time to shut it down. And as for you Doc, your going to be taken out of the mix altogether. You are to live in a tent away from the battalion living area until Topp returns." I was to be completely removed like a bad apple. I couldn't blame them.

The tent was set up behind the HQ building almost on the flight line. The only thing worse than the noise was the sandstorms rolling through the tent. It was full of holes and didn't have a lock on the door. It wasn't operational for any black market affairs, so business declined a bit, but I didn't let it get my spirits down. These two weeks would be a breeze; all I had to do was wait for Topp to get back, and I would be back in business.

Another thing about Sgt. Joe was that he ordered a basewide manhunt for Chip's firearm, a firearm that he neglected to be responsible for. As every available soldier, including me, was out searching for Chip's weapon, he was trying to attain more flight hours so that he could have the most in the unit. And the punishment that he handed out to Short Stuff in the beginning of our tour he did not fulfill himself. He was quite a piece of work. In fact, he didn't apologize or say thank you to anyone; hell, I didn't hear him say a fucking word about it again.

I did my two weeks in the tent and was sent back to Fitz Gerald's room. Luckily, I found some holy wine awaiting some of the churchgoing, God-fearing soldiers, but I figured I would do. Upon Topp's return, he sent for me. He told me that I would report to Sgt. Buck in the morning for an undermanned detail.

Sgt. Buck: 30ish, 5'10" - VLA Status: Enemy. Morals: Idiot. Buck was a real piece of work, be all you can be type shit. He prided himself on kissing ass and being a tool. He thought he was a hardened soldier because...hell, I don't know why he thought that he was hardened, but he was a thorn in my side. He was the poster child for pro-choice.

Sgt. Buck was in charge of the local nationals (Iraqi contractors) while they worked laying sandbags or digging ditches or any other thing that the Americans were too lazy to do, but it wasn't all bad; it put money in their pockets and, hopefully, boosted the economy as a whole. As for us, well, Sgt. Buck just stood behind them and kept his rifle at the low ready, and I found a place out of the sun to come up with catchy one liners to use on Sgt. Buck.

As much as I heard that the Iraqi men were lazy and the women did most of the work, they actually turned out to be hard workers, busting their asses for eight to ten hours a day for almost nothing. Some days, they would ask to work longer. Buck would say that they could, but they wouldn't get paid for it, and still they would do it. They hated him, but he never knew it.

"You don't have to like me, but you will respect me!" he would tell them.

He thought of them as second-class humans, putting them on water breaks during allotted times instead of at their discretion. He would yell at them as a mother would children, and all but one were older than the both of us. Sometimes, Topp would give Buck Kool-Aid to give to the contractors. Buck would of course pass it off for himself.

"Don't say I never gave you nothing." He'd comment.

Within the first week, I was friends with the whole crew. I knew them all by first names but always had to speak through the two translators, Imed and Hyadar. I knew how many wives they all had and their names. I knew their children's names and gave them gifts whenever I could get my hands on them. I took a picture from the oldest man there, Papa. It was a beautiful picture of his daughter, and I told him that he could consider me as a son and her as my sister. The crew got a good laugh after it was translated, and we all began calling him Papa.

At first, their lunch wasn't very appealing to me, as I had gotten used to the number one ranked dining facility in Iraq, but before each meal they would ask me to join them, and each time that I said no there was a look of serious disappointment. Breaking bread with them was the truest sign of friendship. It's like asking someone to stand in your wedding. During the second week, I decided, against orders, to sit down with them. Eating with them was the ultimate way of learning their culture. We all sat Indian style in a large circle facing inwards. Each man would bring one bag or sack with one certain type of food in it; one would bring the humus bread (like pita bread), one with hamburger rolled into marble-size balls, one with potato-log squares, and each had a small leather sack of salt. Then each would use their hands to pick off of the plates and eat it down to their first knuckle, and without hesitation, reach right back into the plates with dripping fingers until all was empty. It took me a minute to pick up this nasty habit and a couple months to pick up tuberculosis. That's right, when I finally returned to the States, I was diagnosed with TB, and the only thing that I could blame it on was swapping spit with the guys. It's alright, it was taken care of, and I wouldn't have traded one bite. In fact, even when I was removed from the detail, I still continued to join them for lunch.

My relationship with Buck continued on a downward spiral. I didn't like speaking with him at all, and he was always asking, "What you thinkin' 'bout?" My answers ranged from, "When your wife is going to leave you," to "How to keep you from reproducing without touching your nuts." Our bonding wasn't going so well, but the Iraqi nationals kept my head on straight.

Two days before I was to be sent back to the hospital from the detail, Moto came to me and said he had a surprise for me. By the time I had gotten to his trailer, the crowd was so thick I could barely make it through the people. Moto cleared a path for me, and before I could see over all the heads, I could smell the booze and hear the confusion of gambling. When I finally made it to the front, someone forced my hand open with a pair of dice. These sons of bitches had built a perfect replica of a craps table, colored carpet and all. I'm not sure where the supplies came from. I sure as hell didn't make any deals, but it did make me realize that Moto wouldn't fail my reputation when I was gone. It was time to bring him to the Green Zone and open the liquor market up for him. I told him that night that that weekend I would set up the flight for Moto, Dave, and me to go to Baghdad. We celebrated the rest of that night until the early morning, and I woke up in one of the Hawaiian girl's bedroom an hour after I was supposed to meet Buck for work.

Running a mile to the HQ was quite a feat with combat equipment, but still being drunk made it nearly impossible. By the time I made it to the pickup site, my hands were on my knees and I was gasping for air. Luckily, as my lungs were being purged of the night's smoke and alcohol, none other than Cpt. Chip showed up to stand above me.

"What, are you late?"

"I missed my ride, but he should have picked up the Iraqis already and be on his way back."

"That's not what I asked. In fact, Buck came and got me this morning right when he realized you were late, and I smell alcohol. Have you been drinking?"

"No, I quit last night."

"I'm sending you to the Combat Army Support Hospital across base; they'll test your blood for alcohol, and you'd better hope that you're clean."

"Great, thank you, you're the best."

Buck was looking for a way to fuck me, and I might as well have been sitting in a Singapore sling. Can't say that I blame him, but usually lower enlisted handle their own problems. Truthfully, if he would have made a comment about my being late, I probably would have said something catchy like, "Go fuck your mother," or "Put a dick in it, Buck," so maybe his best option was to run to the captain. Nonetheless, they had me in a hell of a pickle. I obviously didn't study hard enough for the blood test, because I failed the shit out of it. With the test results in, the command had clearance for an immediate room search.

On the walk there, I couldn't exactly remember what percentage of the liquor was in my room and what the percentage was in the storage room, so when Chip raised the question, "What are we going to find in there?" I said, "Take a guess."

"I'm tired of your mouth. Now you're in a lot of trouble, so..." "I think there's a gallon onside my bed, another couple in my locker. I'm sure I'm forgetting about some, but it won't be hard to find."

When I opened the door, it was obvious I wasn't trying to hide anything. Bottles were all over. As he started collecting them, he noticed one bottle of wine on Fitz Gerald's side.

"Is this yours too, or am I going to have to get Fitz Gerald in here?"

Now, it was his bottle of wine, but he already had me, so there was no reason to bring anyone else into it; besides, they would have never been in the room to find his stash if it weren't for me.

"Everything you find in here belongs to me."

"Even this, is this wine?" he asked, pointing to Fitz Gerald's large collection of piss bottles.

"I don't know," I said as I put my hands over my eyes.

Sure enough, he picked up one of the bottles, unscrewed the cap, and put his nose as far as he could into the bottle and took a whiff. When I started laughing, even Topp couldn't help himself; he covered his mouth and walked outside. Chip shook his head, put the bottle down, and before leaving he added, "You both are fucking disgusting."

It took a couple of days for them to write up the Article 15, and by that time Arilious and I had already discussed my legal options; there were none, plead guilty. Luckily, Chip didn't have the privilege of reading it out to me because he had taken his R&R the day before. So the deed was passed down to The Lieutenant. The funny thing was that it was the first one of his military career. As he was reading it out to me, his hand began to shake, so I covered his hand with mine and winked at him. "Hey, calm down... we're going to get through this." Arilious and I just looked at each other. I didn't have a copy in front of me, but due to my extensive knowledge of Article 15s, I realized at one point he also skipped a sentence.

"I think you missed something there, Lieutenant. Go back a couple of sentences."

Arilious couldn't believe that I was helping him give me the proper fuck, so when The Lieutenant asked if I would like to be advised by my lawyer, Arilious shook his head and told me to step outside.

"Don't help him. If he messes this up, it's possible to use it against him later."

"I know, Arilious, but I feel sorry for him."

Arilious just laughed. "Alright, before we go back in there, I'm not sure what's going to happen to you, and I need a couple of bottles for tonight."

"Here's a key to the storage room; whatever you need, it's on the house."

"Alright, let's get back in there."

When all was finished, they decided on a couple of countermeasures to combat my leadership of the VLA. The first was that I would move back into the tent behind the HQ. The second was that I had to wake up and report every hour on the hour from 6:00 p.m. to 6:00 a.m. to the flight ops, which had soldiers working around the clock, and sign a clock-in sheet. The third was extra duty for my remaining time in Iraq, and fourth, I was to be taken off Buck's detail and put on one across the base.

Here's what they didn't count on. Two days later, Sgt. Joe and Topp bartered for a full-size swimming pool that could only be placed onside the HQ five feet from my tent. Topp bartered for an air conditioning unit that he helped me install along with a wooden door that locked, and he even gave me keys to the HQ, where the phone reached the States and the Internet was always vacant. Within a week, the tent became better than the trailers ever were. Either Giff or Breezy worked the night shift at the flight ops, so they would either bring me the paper to sign or sign it themselves. Once again, when night fell, they lost accountability of me, but that would be the last time they would make this mistake. And as for working across base, I was with a VLA member. I truly thought I was untouchable.

I had visitors every night to do some drinking or smoke weed. Arilious would come every night to discuss operations, present and future. Knight Ryder would come to flaunt the girls he had found and usually to share, and the others to have a drink before retiring for bed.

There is one thing I wanted to add about Knight Ryder. Earlier in the tour, he had met the dental assistant, who was a publicly proclaimed virgin. Although everyone had told him to leave it be and let it go, he persisted. Soon, and I mean real soon, he had gotten to her. Shortly after that they moved in together and became a lot like husband and wife. When he came back from his R&R, he had a bit of a problem. He married his long-time girlfriend, Michelle. With that, the girl had to move back to her room, and they hardly talked afterwards, but Knight Ryder had no intentions to stop there. The girl everyone came to know as the sexy voice of Baghdad was next on his list. No one had seen her, but she was the radio traffic controller when we flew into the Green Zone. A week after he got married, he woke me up with a beautiful girl sitting beside him in my tent.

"Is this a present for me?"

"No, this one's for me. You might know her as the sexy voice of Baghdad."

"Really, finally we meet."

"Yeah, I told her all about you, and I just wanted her to meet you."

"Well, it's my pleasure, honey."

"Listen, I need a favor. I'd like her to spend the night here, maybe throw a party."

He was amazing. He was willing to ruin our black-market flight operation for a piece of ass. He was willing to lie to two commands on two different bases for this girl. In my mind, I went through the steps we'd have to take to make this happen: contact her unit after the last flight had already left for Baghdad; have one of our flight ops personnel lie about why she wasn't on an earlier flight; have one of our housing officers tell her command that they were setting up a place for her to sleep; schedule a flight in the morning for Baghdad and make sure she was on it; get her a uniform from a unit on base, but not one of our own; and last but not least, make sure she didn't open her mouth when she got back. It could be done, but it wasn't going to be easy. Luckily, Knight Ryder told me the good news. They were actually just returning from a weekend vacation in Qatar, one privilege that was taken away from me because of my actions. With this new revelation, I told him all they needed was for someone in her unit who was on vacation with her to tell her command that the C-130 airplane was full and that they scheduled her a flight on a helicopter the next day. We would schedule the flight, and when she returned the next day, no one would be the wiser.

"I told you he would know what to do," Knight Ryder told her with a smile on his face.

That night, he told me that he thought he really liked her and wanted to see her when he made it back to the States. Everyone can justify hating a womanizer, but not a womanizer who thinks he's in love every time. That's why I loved him. He didn't let a little thing like a recent marriage stop him from falling in love. He still makes me smile when I think about him. As a side note, two weeks after he returned home he impregnated a third woman out of wedlock and was divorced shortly after.

Anyway, all was good in the world, and things were about to get better, or the illusion of better.

Chapter Thirteen

Come One, Come Nepal

One night, Arilious and Kenny came to me with good news. The Nepalese contractors Kenny worked with in the dining facility had invited most of the VLA officers over for what I think was like their Fourth of July party. They told me that there would be liquor and even some Nepalese women. *Funny,* I thought, *I know the Nepalese aren't getting liquor from me, and I can't imagine men making only $250 a year could be buying it from my competitors.* I had to check it out. They were set in a fenced-off camp around two miles away from the soldiers' trailers. As we walked up, I witnessed a party like I have never seen before, either in Iraq or in the States. There were no women, but every man was dancing in a circle surrounding one younger boy. When we walked up, the dancing continued, but each man kindly shook our hands with a half bow. With this they would usually offer us anything from food to a place to sleep if we needed it. Since that day, I was hooked.

The only one who spoke half-assed English was a twenty-five-ish-year-old man by the name of Ashok, pronounced ah-soak. He was a good looking young man who loved playing the guitar. He tried to translate everything that was being said to us, but sometimes he just waved them off if it was too ridiculous to translate. Ashok lived in a room that was actually larger than the soldiers' trailers, but there were six to ten men living in it with him. While we were at the party, I asked where they were getting the whiskey from. He explained that there were nightly trades over the fence with the Iraqis. He went on to tell me that the liquor was endless. He could get me whatever I'd like for ten dollars a bottle as long as it was made in Lebanon. Lebanon, besides producing terrorists, also produces some of the world's worst whiskey. With names like *Black Man, Black Horse, Three Horses,* and *Kasandra,* which would soon be a favorite around base, it would be hard to compete with American brands...unless there were no American products left coming in.

When the sales of alcohol started, there were three main distributors. The other two could fly personally to the Green Zone three times a week due to their work schedule. On the other hand, I had to depend on many men to go for me, and they would take their cut as they saw fit. The VLA was the most spread out, of course, and better known, but the truth is we were the third in the amount distributed. The plan of action I decided to take would give me a bad name to some, a traitor's name, but it would be good for the VLA in the long run.

When Chip arrived back from his R&R, I scheduled a meeting with him. He had asked me more times than I could remember where I was getting the liquor from. Well, I was ready to tell him.

"Yes, sir, in hopes of maybe gaining some of my privileges back, I'd like to discuss the alcohol that was found in my room."

"What's there to discuss?"

"Where we're getting it from."

"We? Who's we?"

"Everyone, sir. Ever since the battalion commander opened up flights to priority personnel, everyone became priority. Six, seven, eight soldiers a day are returning from the Green Zone with bags full of liquor. The flight crews don't know because we're on and off before they are."

"The Green Zone. That's where everything's coming from?"

"Yes, sir."

"Well, I'm going to do all I can to help you out, but I can't promise anything."

He wasn't going to lift a finger to help me out. His head grew with thoughts of winning the battle between him and me. He thought of eight privates carrying him around in a princess' carriage. Wonderful fantasies filled his head of working out in a loin cloth while a crowd gathered to applaud, but while he was sucking up victory, he played himself right into my hands. It took him two days to cancel all non-helicopter crew personnel flights, which meant no one was getting their asses out of Balad except for the men who worked outside of Balad, in turn meaning no more liquor from the Green Zone. Victory! With the Nepalese bartering for all the liquor we would ever need, VLA became the sole distributor of alcohol on base.

While I mainly worked through three loyal VLA officers, I couldn't estimate how far our market ran. I bought for ten sold for twenty, they bought for twenty and sold for thirty, and a ways down the line people were buying regularly for one hundred a bottle. The four of us made a substantial amount of money on liquor. As for marijuana, I quit it all together. I now worked in hashish. Just think of a black tootsie roll that sold for two hundred dollars. Pure THC. I received it regularly through the translator I had met through the Iraqi contractors. I would send someone on the first of the week to meet him in the restroom during one of Sgt. Buck's allotted restroom breaks. I'd buy four tootsie rolls a week for fifty a pop and sell for two hundred. Soon, the Hawiians had me buying ten a week. This profit I kept for myself...you know, for rainy days.

With things running smoothly again, I sighed with relief knowing that we only had another month and a half before our advanced party left for Kuwait. I actually thought I might get out of that country with more money as a private than Chip would as a captain. Hell, if I played my cards right, I might end up with an honorable discharge. But at that point, my discharge was the least of my worries.

The Nepalese became the VLA's number one allies. Every night, Arilious and I and usually some others would visit them for a drink. Ashok would play the guitar and talk about his home, and we would sing and talk about ours. We began to learn their language and know their names. We even spent some nights watching Nepalese movies, which I could barely understand, but I enjoyed them anyway. We talked about going to Nepal to meet their families and finding work visas so that maybe they could come work and live with us in the U.S. They became true friends. We would have chosen them over most of our own American colleagues.

One night, I decided to stay in and catch up on some sleep while Arilious went to make a pick-up from the Nepalis. When he got back, I knew something was wrong.

"Get up!"

I never questioned him. I was on my feet and throwing my pants on.

"We've got a problem. I just need you as muscle."

"Should we get Big Vin?"

"No, this has to stay between me and you."

As we walked into the entrance gate of the Nepalese camp, instead of making a right to Ashok's room, he made a left. The trailer that he was going to had a sign with Nepalese words, then large words in English: "Contract Manager." Now, since the soldiers weren't supposed to be back there in the first place, I didn't see what we had to do with the boss of the Nepalese. Arilious slung open the door as if it were a hundred pounds, and I grabbed it from behind him before it could come slamming back. There were two fat men sitting across the desk from each other, and both their faces quickly turned to us. The fat man on the opposite side of the desk was the first to speak, although in broken English.

"How may I help you?"

I kept silent, but Arilious was furious. "Who's the manager?" The man in the roll-back office chair raised his hand.

"Then you can leave," Arilious said, looking at the guy on our side.

The fat guy just sat there with a puzzled look on his face. All Arilious had to do was turn his head in my direction, and I knew what he was saying loud and clear. I pulled his seat out from under the desk and whispered, "Get the fuck out!"

As the fat man exited, Arilious turned back to the manager.

"This is a list of names of the men who are leaving tomorrow," he said, slapping a piece of paper on the desk.

"These men cannot leave. They are under contract."

"Yeah, that's another thing; their contract is void as of right now. They owe you no money, and you owe them no money. I am a legal advisor for the United States Army, and there are so many violations on your part, it would be in your best interest to release these men and not get any further publicity on the subject."

"These men have never come to me with such a problem."

"Again, not my problem. They stopped working for you over three weeks ago because they think you're a tyrant. Now you're not allowing them to leave their rooms, not even for food. They're going home tomorrow."

"When I contact the Baghdad International Airport, it still sometimes takes months to get a flight. Please, I will let them go, but it will take some time." the fat man rebuttled.

"Have their release papers here tomorrow at 0600 (6:00 a.m). Do you understand?"

"Yes. I understand."

Walking out the door, I was dumbfounded. This was the first I'd ever heard of any of this. Ashok never told me he had stopped going to work or that the boss was a tyrant. I knew that the contracting company paid two thousand dollars for each man sent, and every man sent made twenty-five hundred dollars in two years, so that after their dues were paid, each man would go home with five hundred dollars after two years. Yeah, it sucked, but it was more than the average Nepali made back home. I'm not sure what clearances Arilious had to do this, but I could almost bet that he had none and he let his emotions get the best of him.

"What the fuck are you doing?"

"Ashok and two other guys want to go home, and I'm sending them."

"Do you have the clearance to do this?"

"Look who's talking. Do you have clearances to do anything?"

"Go'dammit, Arilious, this do-gooder bullshit can get us into more trouble than I ever brought on us."

"We're fighting a war to free people, Doc, and yet there are slaves right under our noses. This is what we're here for. You are always talking about doing more for the cause. This is it...I need your help, please."

After a short pause, I said, "Of course, you never had to ask. I'm just saying we have to be real low key about this."

His plan wasn't exactly worked out. We would take Ashok and the other two to one of the vacant trailers that I still had a key to. They would stay there that night to avoid any intimidation tactics, or worse. The next day, he would personally escort the men on a flight to the airport and try to get them on the plane. Without the needed clearances, he wouldn't get past scaring the shit out of the manager. So it was time to go to work. Arilious brought the guys to collect their shit, and I went to Breezy to schedule the flight. When he saw the names, he looked up with questions. Before he could say anything, I just put my head in my hand and shook it up and down, just telling him to do it but keep it low key. Arilious went to one of the officers who owed the VLA a favor; this certain officer contacted BIAP (Baghdad International Airport) and, without any questions, we had a flight to Nepal. To tie everything together the next morning, the release papers were handed right over. The son of a bitch did it; he took all of our connections and got three men back to their families and away from this crazy world. I knew from that point, when he wanted something done, it was going to be done.

When Ashok left, he told us to trust one of his good friends, Adidas Son. Adidas Son would be able to handle our future endeavors, whether it was alcohol, Nepali parties, or just a friend. He couldn't speak English very well, but we all picked up on Nepali, and together we had enough to get by.

Chapter Fourteen

The Infamous Night in Question

A couple days after the Nepalis were sent home, I received some startling news. As I walked in to the flight ops building for my first sign-in, I saw the chaplain standing there all smiles.

"Hey, Doc, how's it going?"

"You know me, sir. Pregnant women and coat hangers, business as usual."

"You son of a bitch, you're going straight to hell."

Now, hearing that I was going to hell wasn't unusual, but it was from a priest. I didn't see it coming. To think of it now, priests usually have to tell the truth, and he probably was.

"How's your new guest?" he added before he walked out.

"What guest?"

With that he was gone, and I was off to check the tent for anything that wasn't supposed to be there. When I opened the unlocked door, I saw three cots lined up next to mine, three piles of clothes with gear on top, and finally three men rifling through my liquor cabinet. The three men were a troublesome bunch from a different company. One had been busted with eight hundred pills of ecstasy, and the other two had been busted for doing it with him. These men were known as the White Devils.

White Devils: no affiliation with the VLA. The name was bestowed on them by an Iraqi translator. They were three helicopter mechanics with luck for shit. Almond was the only one with balls, Richy was the only one with any sense, and the Rat was a young low-down snitch.

I'd seen these men around but had never spoken to them. I decided to welcome them with a couple bottles of whiskey and sit down to hear their story. Apparently, the Rat smuggled eight hundred X pills through three countries by storing them in a candle jar and melting the wax around them. When he was finally busted, instead of telling the Criminal Investigation Department (CID) that he had a drug problem and was planning to take them all, he said he was planning to sell them and gave up the names of the buyers. Can you imagine the interrogators when he told them he was planning to sell the pills? They must have taken pictures with him and brought in friends, called the people back home. "Hey, Mom, listen to this fucking idiot." He was too stupid to be in the game he was in. Which brings us to Almond, who when questioned about it, agreed to take a blood test and was busted for buying and using. Richy told CID to suck on a love stick and was probably going to get away with just living in a tent for the remaining time. The other two were looking at jail time. They were a little stupid, but they were my kind of company, all but the Rat.

As I sat around listening to them tell stories of their families back home, two bottles of whiskey were killed. I decided to take a walk with the Rat over to the Nepali camp to pick up a couple more bottles. I figured it was a good time to explain that everyone's entitled to one mistake; his mistake wasn't the drugs, it was ratting himself and his friends out. Obviously, his friends weren't too upset about it since we had just finished two bottles of whiskey, and he wasn't dead yet. So I told him he was entitled to no more; if he ever thought about using my operation as a pawn to get out of his trouble, I'd put him in the dining facility disposal pit. I thought he understood what I was saying, but once a rat always a rat. So I left him at Adidas Son's room while Adidas Son and I went to retrieve the whiskey from our storage room.

When the Rat and I returned to the tent, neither of the other two were there. Now, not that I wasn't worried about these two fools running around drunk, bringing attention to me, but I'm no go'damn babysitter. I wasn't going out looking for them. I put the bottle aside and prepared for bed. By the time my head hit the pillow, I was asleep. I was awakened by the other two White Devils returning. In their hands were weapons, but not that that was peculiar, everyone had guns. By the time my mind caught up with what was going on, I realized their weapons had been taken away when they were accused with drug charges; these weapons were stolen from someone. This was all I needed. I jumped up and threw my BDU bottoms on. The Rat told me they were on their way back to the other unit to take more guns to add to the six stolen weapons that were already in my tent. The Rat hadn't done anything wrong yet, so I felt bad about taking it out on him, but I jumped in his face, showed my teeth, and let him know in a way that he could understand.

"Get those fucking things out of my tent."

I was furious. They'd compromised my operation in every way, and I definitely didn't need any more attention. I ran to where the Rat thought they were, and I saw two soldiers with flashlights.

"Hey, you two."

But when they turned around, I knew I was fucked. It was two men from the other company; they were looking into a conex that was acting as an armory. The sons of bitches stole guns from an American armory. They were as surprised to see me as I was to see them.

"Sorry, fellows, I'm looking for two other guys."

"Wait, hold on. They have two guys running around out here?"

"I don't know." They both knew I was lying.

"Soldier, we're missing weapons from this armory, and if you know something, you'd better tell me before we have our command get involved."

"Look, man, I don't know."

"What's your name?"

I used my first name because if I had used my last name, they would have realized who I was.

"Are you back here with anyone else?" they asked.

"My roommates are in the tent behind our HQ right back there."

"Do you mind if we go talk to them?"

"I don't give a fuck what you do."

"Well, can you lead the way?"

With a deep sigh, I just put my head down and started to walk. When we all made it back to the tent, all three White Devils were there and doing their best to act like they were sleeping.

"Do you mind if we search around this tent?"

"If you're looking for guns...no, I don't care, but for anything else you come across..."

"We don't care about anything else, just guns."

"Be my guest."

As they were stripping the tent, I realized that they didn't want to report it; they would be in just as much trouble as we would be. They left an armory unlocked and open and now were missing guns. They were fucked if they didn't find these things tonight.

"Do you mind if we wake them up?"

"Yeah, I do. I have to get ready for work, and you can talk to them in the morning."

They wrote down the information that I gave them and left. I walked them out to make sure they would be far enough away before I woke these sons of bitches up.

"Where are the guns?" I demanded, with one hard slap to the Rat's face.

"What?"

"The guns. Don't worry, I'm not going to tell them."

"I took them to the camp you took me to earlier."

Americans stealing weapons can be played off as a joke, but when they end up at a foreign contractor's room who is known for bartering with the Iraqis. It's very serious, and that's how I took it. Without saying a word and still without my shirt on, I ran the whole two miles, and not just ran, I ran as hard as I could. They were my friends, and I betrayed them by bringing over that bastard who didn't care about them at all. They didn't know any better. They figured if I brought him over, then he probably brought the guns over for me. At that point, I realized that I didn't care if the White Devils were busted for this; I just had to keep the Nepalese out of it. By the time I made it to the door, I was so excited that I ripped the lock off. As the door came off the hinges, eight scared faced turned my way, but fear quickly turned to relief when they saw that it was me. Out of breath, I tried my best to remain calm. I felt so strongly then that my eyes are watering just thinking about it now.

"Adidas Son, listen to me, never take anything from anyone unless it's me. This is very bad; you have to explain to everyone here never to talk about this again." I couldn't stop myself from crying, but I continued. They knew I was serious then.

"If they know that you had these, you can go to prison. Never tell anyone. I'll be back tomorrow to explain." I gave one of those hugs that no one could deny, and I left.

While I was on my way back, I thought that I might be able to return the weapons and that this nightmare would be over. During this fantasy, I realized that the company from which the weapons were stolen was lit up like a candle. It's not hard to see extra lights in the desert. CID was there already; this situation just got out of my hands. I was going to bring the guns back and tell the story, minus the Nepalese camp, but then I realized that if I put the Rat on the stand, he would definitely come clean about everything, even Adidas Son. I couldn't let that happen. I made an executive criminal decision. I began to break down the guns piece by piece and toss them into the dining facility disposal pit. I only finished the first one when a Humvee turned down the path I was on; it could have been anyone, but I wasn't sticking around to find out. I threw all of the guns in whole and ran the back path to the soldiers' trailers.

Thank the Lord that Knight Ryder never locked his door. I woke him up, obviously out of breath. He asked me what was wrong.

"I can't explain now. I need a shirt and a blouse."

"My blouse says my name on it."

"I don't care."

He gave me the shirt, and I was out the door by sunrise. I met my ride, and we left to do some work on the other side of base. It was obvious that I had been up all night, but that happened at least twice a week, so no one was the wiser. I worked with a VLA member, so he let me sleep most of the day, but right after lunchtime, I received an expected phone call. Topp was on his way over to pick me up; apparently there had been some investigators from CID who had questions for me. At that time, I figured I was the only one they had information on, the only one found at the scene of the crime, so I was the only one they would question. Unless I gave up a lead, they had nothing, and I was as quiet as high school bedroom sex at her mother's house.

During the ride, Topp apologized for sticking those assholes with me and assured me that I wasn't a suspect. Once he apologized, I knew that they were questioning the White Devils, so if I wasn't a suspect now, I would be when they broke one of those amateurs.

When I walked into the conference room of our battalion headquarters, there stood a five foot nothing black woman and a very large, white, young buck waiting for me. They directed me to sit on the opposite side of the table from them. I told them I'd rather stand. In fact, here's some advice for all: if the people asking you to sit are standing, don't. It's a way to intimidate you. Something about the human psyche makes you intimidated by anything higher than you. The young buck got straight to business.

"Sit!"

"What is this about?" I asked while leaning over the table.

"Where were you last night?"

"If this is about the weapons..."

"Who said anything about weapons?"

"I did. Two men explained to me last night that there were some missing weapons. In fact, they came and searched my tent."

"What were you doing over there?"

"Getting accountability. Three men were put in my tent; when I woke up, only one was there. I went to look for the other two."

"Where were they?"

"I don't know. I guess in the bathroom. When I returned with the other guys, they were in bed sleeping."

"Why aren't you wearing rank, soldier?"

"Why aren't you?" I rebuttled.

"We don't because sometimes we have to interrogate higher ranking personnel. We don't want rank getting in the way of an investigation."

"I don't wear rank because I don't want it to get in the way of sex."

"I'm sorry, you are the man they call Doc right?"

"I am."

"And yet your blouse says Knight Ryder."

"It's a long story, but if this is all a mistake and you actually meant to interrogate him, then I know where he is."

"They said you were smooth. We're going to bring you down to the station; we have a couple more questions for you."

The young buck came to my side of the table, I guess to make sure I didn't run. Seriously, where the hell was I going to go? When we got to the station, I was handed off to a smaller fellow who was a real talkative prick. Not knowing that I was a suspect, he began to explain some of the recent crimes committed on base. They were nothing compared to what I did every day. He then began to explain some of the techniques used to get someone to talk. As I listened and went over the story in my head, we made our way to the interrogation building. I took the last drag of my cigarette and tossed it into a vacant corner. Past that corner and over the hedges, I saw my world crumble. The Rat was in tears, being questioned by the same unranked black woman. When we finally locked eyes, he let out a loud, high-pitched "Fuck!" and then fell to the ground. It was time for self-preservation; anything I said in the small, windowless room would be held against me in court. So I locked up. I explained that before I made a statement I wanted to see a lawyer. I signed a couple of papers that had Knight Ryder's name on it, and they threw me in a holding cell.

All four of us were in consecutive holding cells. We didn't share a word until Sgt. Maj. arrived and requested to see me outside. I know how it looked to everyone, and Almond let me know it. "You motherfucker!" I wished I could turn around and tell them, "We all know who the snitch is, so don't motherfucker me." But indicating that there was a rat would be indicating that there was a crime, and since we were all upset about there being a snitch, it would be an admission of our part in the crime. So I silently followed Sgt. Maj. out the door.

"I'm going to try this once. It's time for damage control. If you know anything about what happened last night, you'd better tell me."

"Sorry, Sgt. Maj., I told them what I know."

Then he lost it. "You motherfucker! We were on the same team, and you fucked me. I tried to help you. Now you're gonna go down with these three bastards."

"That's the second time in five minutes I've been called motherfucker. Now she's not here to defend herself, so I'd appreciate if you didn't say it again."

I knew he wasn't going to back down, but what I didn't see coming was a staring contest. With his eyes he said, "I understand that I'm old and you're young, but if I wasn't worried about losing my rank, I'd quench your thirst with that pavement." And my eyes were saying, "If you hit me, they'd probably sweep this whole thing under the rug."

"Get in the fucking truck...in the back."

Once I got back across base, I was ordered to go to my tent and wait there. There were no charges pressed on us yet, but I figured it wouldn't be long. I decided to do some damage control of my own. I readied for a shower as cover and went straight to Arilious' trailer. He was still ignorant of the situation, but when I told his roommate to get the fuck out, he realized something was wrong. I told him the story exactly how I told it here and sat while he went into cover-up mode.

"Collect everyone who was involved and anyone who might know."

"I'm pretty sure one of them rolled over; if that's true, you don't want to be anywhere near this, Arilious."

"You're in trouble, so I'm already in it."

I quickly found out that we were all separated so as not to coordinate stories. Just as quickly, I found out where each one was and rounded them up at the tent. Arilious sat us down and painted us a picture. It was the last-minute effort of desperate men, but if we could pull it off, it might work. In this meeting, I learned that there had been another rifle stolen on the second trip, and it had been thrown into a huge sand crate five feet from the tent. The plan was to retrieve all the weapons before anyone else, clean the prints, anonymously return them to Arilious' legal office, and most importantly, say nothing to CID or the command.

As a whole, Arilious, the White Devils, and I went to the DFAC disposal pit and dug through month-old food and daily table scraps. It was trying on everyone. We all began to bicker and threaten each other. I expressed my feelings about the Rat and my desire to leave him buried in the pit, and even I was blamed for dismantling one of the weapons and tossing it into the pit. Their reasoning was that they would only get in trouble if all the weapons weren't returned. The situation worsened with every minute we were in there. One weapon, two weapons, get down helicopter over head. Finally we found all of the whole weapons and began looking for cigarette-sized pieces of the dismantled weapon. Finally, the situation was too much to bear, and I found myself standing toe-to-toe with Almond. I wanted nothing more than to kill all three of those fucks then and there, but Arilious had startled us with something we missed.

"You two, shut up! The other weapon... they're going to begin searching around the tent first; we have to get it out of the sand crate. We'll take what we have back, and hopefully that'll be good enough, but we have to get that other gun away from the tent."

With that said, we all broke away to our respective places. I sent Almond to retrieve the gun from the sand crate, I went to tell Knight Ryder that I never came in that night to borrow a shirt, and Arilious went to his office to clean the fingerprints off the guns we had. When I returned to the tent, I was met by a major in our unit.

"Didn't they tell you to stay in the tent?"

"I was taking a shower."

Apparently, the word spread, and all of my enemies were looking for the missing weapons. After speaking with me, the major climbed into the sand crate in his search. He began jumping from one to the other and, finally, into the one where the weapon was hidden. I lost my breath. I didn't know if Almond listened or if he hadn't gotten to it yet or what. The major dug around for a second and then leaped out. If he had come five minutes before, he would have found a weapon with one of the White Devil's fingerprints on it, which in turn would have drawn out a confession, and of course my tour would become a lot longer.

That night, I didn't sleep a wink. Arilious went to his office and wiped the fingerprints clean. Later, he told me that getting the prints off of every piece took him all night. Like me, he would do no dreaming that night. The next morning, they found six and a half weapons leaning on the legal office door in a duffle bag with no name on it. I'm not sure what the note said that was left with the weapons, but obviously it pissed them off more.

Chapter Fifteen

Arilious, Above and Beyond the

Call of Brotherhood

The next morning, I was directed to stay in my tent until they knew what to do with me. It was the calm before the storm. I lay around reading the books my family had sent me, thinking about them, thinking of how disappointed my father would be and how worried my mother would be. I thought about Hollie and how much volunteering for this war hurt her and now me. Idle time in Iraq is the worst thing a soldier can go through. It's not the hospital and people dying, it's not the shooting or being shot at, it's the *time* that kills your mind slowly, the thoughts of what could have been and what could be. It's enough to make a man start drinking; in fact, I had a bottle left from a couple nights before, and that's exactly what I started doing. By the time Topp walked in, I didn't give a shit about anything.

"You probably know this already, but they found the weapons."

"Oh yeah?"

"They're still pressing charges."

"That's not unexpected."

"Your orders are as follows. You are to relinquish your weapon until the end of the trial. You are to be placed under armed escort at all times, lunch, showers, bathroom, even while you sleep. Everyone included in the charges are not allowed to speak with each other, and you will be given a lawyer from Baghdad, so you can't even speak with Arilious. Somehow he was pulled into this fuck fest."

That was exactly what I was worried about, someone rolled on Arilious. I needed to find out who went back to CID today, that would be the informant.

"Arilious is being questioned now. Almond and Richy are under the same treatment as you, and the escorts know not to put you all together, and the other one is being flown to Baghdad today to await his trial. Apparently, he's said something to make them think that one of you would make an attempt on his life."

"Oh yeah? Well, who's my lucky escort?"

"I'm taking you to his room right now; gather up your shit."

On the ride to meet my escort, all I could think about was that rat bastard. They had probably released him last night to find out where I had put the weapons. Not only did he find that out, but I also drug Arilious into the mess right in front of his eyes. That little bastard knew everything, everything. There was no chance of us getting out of this together; soon, there would be plea bargains made, and Arilious and I didn't stand a chance against three of them making the same accusations. I was trying to compute the physical evidence they had, which I thought was none, and the eyewitness testimonies, which I couldn't get around. I wasn't computing fast enough. I tried to wake up from this nightmare, but before I could I was at my escort's trailer.

"Sgt. Buck, that's who you're putting me with? Buck. Topp, I'm going through enough shit right now; don't put me with this asshole."

"I don't want to hear it; you'll do as he says. Understood?"

Buck just returned from a meeting with all the first sergeants who explained to him that I should be in a cell, so I didn't need any privileges that I wouldn't have in jail. He took that to the extreme. The power got to his little pea head. He didn't allow me to watch movies, write on my laptop, read books, or have visitors. I was to work with him every day from 8:00 a.m. to 8:00 p.m. with the crew of Iraqi nationals, except this time I wasn't guarding them; this time I was doing whatever they were doing. My back was getting strong after a week of filling and throwing sandbags, digging ditches, and whatnot. The Iraqi crew noticed that I couldn't keep up with them and began taking the shovel from me; they didn't allow me to throw any sandbags even at the expense of Buck yelling and lifting his gun as if he would shoot them. I began to love them bastards and they me. One day Imed came to me and asked, "Why is Buck being like this to you?"

"I did bad things."

"No, not you. We love you. We do not love Buck. Do you want us to...kill him?"

He had a dead serious face until I began to laugh. Then they all began to laugh as if they had already spoken about doing it. I thankfully declined and gave him a hug.

The next week I went to the DFAC (dining facility) with Buck closely behind. If my goal was to become famous in Iraq, then I certainly didn't disappoint myself. Everyone there knew who I was; everyone was trying to catch a glimpse of me. Each table I walked by would become eerily silent. When I finally made it to the lunch line, Adidas Son handed me a plate and with it a napkin. The napkin simply said, "Number 5 stall, 8:00 p.m., bring a pen." It didn't have a name or a reason, but I knew it was sent down the line until it made it to Kenny or Amy, who were the only two VLA members who worked with Adidas Son in the DFAC. I didn't know whether to expect a blowjob or a bullet, but I knew if someone went through all that trouble to get me that note, then I'd better be there.

Buck had to stand by the bathroom stall door while I went. Although it was embarrassing for me, I knew it was degrading for him, but he followed orders like a good little soldier. When I walked in, I noticed someone in stall number 6. *Must be my mystery date.* I took down my pants, and before I sat down on the toilet, a hand reached under with a pocket notebook and a pen. The conversation that follows was done without a word and was mostly abbreviated.

"It's Arilious. The new prosecutor and his three assistants just flew in today. The Rat rolled on everyone; they won't let you see your lawyer until they've read you your charges formally."

"Is the prosecutor experienced? Is my lawyer experienced? What happened to you?"

"Young, no. Called in a favor for yours, if I can get him he's the best. They're not charging me with anything. They hope to hang you three and to put a fourth denial could hurt the case. I have too much credibility. You three will be easier."

"Good, I'm sorry for everything. Any physical evidence? Will the other two plea?"

"No physical. The other two have been back to CID twice, and their lawyers are on base, so they talk every day. Not looking good."

"What next?"

"Your lawyer will know what their lawyers will have before I will. What he says will determine the next move."

"Thank you for everything. You're a good friend."

"Do you want me to contact your family?"

"No. In fact, I almost forgot. How's the family?"

"He's not good. He's being indicted."

I added the "How's the family?" thing because I always ask him that when I see him. I wanted him to get a laugh out of it; instead, he got a brother out of it. His brush with this investigation should have put him on his knees with his back towards me, but not him; now he's my inside man on the prosecution.

The next day went as a normally as expected with a little twist before dinner. After the Iraqi nationals left, I was still looking at four hours of extra duty. Buck walked me to a pile of sandbags the size of a house. On top of that pile were the two White Devils tossing loaded sandbags into the back of a deuce and a half.

"Don't say a word to each other; just fill up the deuce and a half."

Buck stood watch as the three of us tossed ten-pound bags of sand through the air. We were almost done with the back of the truck when another soldier ran up to Buck. He listened to the soldier's whispers then looked at us.

"I have to go to a meeting. Can I trust you three to finish without saying a word while I go get one of your other escorts from the DFAC?"

I gave the thumbs up, and he was gone. Immediately the three of us began cursing the Rat. I told them to keep throwing sandbags while we talked, not to raise attention. I explained to them that there would be no plea bargains, that the only way to beat the charge was to stick together. As the conversation remained moderately civilized, we continued to throw sandbags. Soon, my point was clear, and the back of the deuce and a half was full. Buck wasn't back yet, so I ordered the White Devils to continue throwing. I told them, "Put em on the roof, the hood; hell, open a door and fill up the cab," and we did. We left just enough room for Buck to fit his skinny little ass in the driver's seat. I know it wasn't the best idea because of all the shit we were in, but anything I could do to bond with these fellows would help. The look on Buck's face was worth whatever they could do to us.

"Whose idea was this?"

"Mine. You told us to fill up the deuce and a half. That's what we did."

"Well, now, all of you can walk behind it and pick up every bag that falls."

When he opened the door to see the inside of the cab was the best. "That's fucking great."

We walked behind the trembling deuce and a half until we made it to the trailer area. When Buck tried to make his way off the road, *boom! boom!* Everyone within a quarter-mile radius dropped to the ground. Everyone thought a mortar round had landed on a trailer, or at least that's what it sounded like. In actuality, two of the tires on the deuce and a half blew out, which is not an easy feat. As people came out to take pictures, the White Devils and I climbed up on the truck like a defeated dragon to wade in victory. We laughed as Buck yelled to the top of his little lungs. We unloaded the truck in record time without losing our smiles. We laughed as we jumped down from the truck.

"Anything else...Buck?"

Looking at the White Devils, he said, "You two fix the tires, and as for you, Doc, come with me."

I knew where he was going the minute he started walking. He only knew one tactic to win, and that was the chain of command. When he opened the door to the HQ, he left the mad, irate Buck outside and tried to regain control.

"Topp, I'm putting in a request for the generator lights."

"Why?"

"The Doc's gonna fill some sandbags on the flight line until midnight."

"What? Why?"

"He just blew the tires out on the deuce and a half by loading the whole thing, even the cab, with sandbags."

I looked at Topp for a laugh but there was none. Topp put his head in his hands like he was actually thinking about Buck's proposition. I figured if I didn't chime in now, the night would have gotten a lot longer.

"Wait, I'm sorry. Is this an attempt to break me?"

When I said it, Buck sent me a message. He gave me one of those grins that says, "There's no attempt about it." I'll admit, I lost my calm. When I jumped over Topp's desk, no one even moved to stop me. I grabbed Buck by his blouse and brought him in for a face-to-face.

"People like you, motherfucker, don't break people like me."

Topp spoke up. "Doc, you're moving. Get all your shit ready. I'll have your new escort come and get you. Buck, we'll take care of the deuce and a half in the morning. If there is nothing else, please get out of my office."

At least I got a new escort out of the deal; hell, I guess I should've been violent all along. I had very little in Buck's room, so by the time my new escort arrived, I was ready.

Big Sgt.: 30ish, 6'4" - VLA Status: Neutral. Morals: High. Big Sgt. was a big teddy bear. He was one of those guys who could make you smile no matter the situation you were in, not because he was funny, but because he was so simple. He would get up to watch the sunrise and talk about how good the morning cup of coffee was all day. If I could be like someone else, it would be him.

He went over the rules that he had to abide by, and other than that he didn't care. I think we enjoyed each other's company because we were so different. He would sit in disbelief as I told him of all of my antics, and I would listen to him as he talked about New Zealand, which he talked about in depth. I figured we'd get along perfectly, but before I could sigh with relief, he was gone. Little did we know that, in a trailer not too far from his, a fight had broken out. The fight was between an E-6 and an E-7, who I guess should have known better, but because they didn't, they were punished with my company. I was with Big Sgt. for two days, and then poof, I was gone.

Sgt. Fish: late 30s, 5'9" - VLA Status: Member. Morals: Low. Fish was a hell of a guy. He loved to have a good time, and everyone knew it. We knew each other from the wine still; his wife was the one who sent the yeast.

Sgt. Stress: mid 40s, 5'11" - VLA Status: Neutral. Morals: Med. Sgt. Stress will probably have had a heart attack by the time anyone lays eyes on this book. He was worried about everything and overworked himself daily. I'll bet back home he was a pretty nice guy, but there he stressed everyone else out.

The duo took me in like I was one of their kids, a drunk, violent, crime-boss kid. They laid down the law quickly. I was their punishment, and that's how they decided to look at it. Before I could start enjoying their warm welcome, there was a knock at the door. It was Arilious.

"You're not an easy guy to find; three rooms in just as many days."

The duo started up. "He's not supposed to talk to you; I'm sorry."

"That's alright; I just stopped by to tell you that his formal charges are being read tomorrow. Bring him to the HQ for 1300 (1:00 p.m.)."

It actually felt good to hear that news, any news for that matter. I was ready to see what I was being charged with. If everything I had done before this was preparation, then this was the war. That night, I was actually excited. I couldn't wait to get in the office. I couldn't wait to see my prosecutor, the enemy. I couldn't wait for him to see me. I thought I was ready, but nothing could prepare me for what was behind the doors of that office. While they were reading my charges, I couldn't take my eyes off of the prosecutor's assistants. They were a nine and ten on the desert scale. By the time they asked me if I understood my charges, I could have been getting an award. "Yes." When I walked out the building, Arilious followed closely.

"Arilious, get me the two assistants."

"That's a serious no-go in the legal world."

"Just get 'em to my room."

Arilious fell behind, and I beelined for the main walkway. I turned around and just before he went into the HQ, I hollered, "And get me to my lawyer!"

That week, the first of our unit began to pack up and ship out. It didn't feel good. It felt like this was all coming to an end for most and just beginning for me. They couldn't even come to tell me bye, but a couple did show up to say hello.

Sgt. Hottie: 25, 5'5". She was almost professional, almost innocent, and almost the girl next door...but not quite. For being Hispanic, she was quiet and nice. She had a sense of goodness that I haven't seen in a long time. She was perfect for the prosecutor's team.

Spc. Sexy: 24, 5'6". She was anti-conscience. She was the reason that Sgt. Hottie would get off the beaten path. She was a smart-ass, vicious, little Latina. She loved to have a good time, and she was my in. She had a fiancé there there with us, but she and I both knew he couldn't hold a candle to me.

Arilious never fails. He pretty much brought them to me with a bow.

"Doc, these girls wanted to meet you."

"They wanted to meet me?"

"Yeah, they said you look like an Abercrombie and Fitch model, not a convict."

That son of a bitch was so good, he made them think that they wanted to meet me. He was my hero. We introduced ourselves, shook hands, and shared a couple of words. They also let me know that they would be escorting me to see my lawyer in Baghdad the next day. Things were moving quicker than I thought.

The next morning, I was escorted to the flight line by my usuals. Once I got there, Arilious used the old, "I'll take it from here, fellows." Arilious said it was approved by the command. To this day, I don't know if it was true or not.

"How's the family, Arilious?"

"Not now, Doc; put these on."

With that, he dropped what looked like forty pounds of shackles.

"Are you serious?"

"Yeah, here I'll help you."

And there it is, back to the beginning of the story. Sorry it took so long. The rest should go by a lot quicker.

Chapter Sixteen

Fuck It, If You Go Down, We're Coming with You

They released me from my shackles when we made it to Baghdad, but not before I made a hell of an entrance. Arilious and I unloaded off of one bird as the prosecutor's assistants unloaded off the other, and the windows in the flight ops building filled up with faces. I'd been to Victory Base before but never under these circumstances. To know in your mind that you're not a criminal but to be treated like one and looked at like one is sort of exhilarating. I can imagine it's the same feeling of a white kid who acts black. Hell, to get that feeling again, I'm thinking about throwing on a wave cap.

We made our way across base toward my lawyer's office as I tried to make headway with Hottie and Sexy. Arilious was constantly in my ear.

"He's the best lawyer in Iraq, but he still works for the Army. The Army's main agenda is not to get any publicity for this. So he was probably ordered to get you to cop a plea. Let him get all of his information from the other statements. He'll tell you he's on your side and ask about what happened, but you can give him nothing. Think of him as the enemy."

Arilious had never failed me yet, so again, I didn't question him.

I forget my lawyer's name, but he was a tall drink of water. Nicely pressed uniform, hair fixed, he was unlike anyone else out there. He had an actual office and not just an old closet that was cleaned up. I think he was a major, but don't quote me on that. He wasn't there for the bullshit, and he threw himself into it before we sat down.

"I would just like to say that I'm not a defense attorney anymore. I don't take cases, and I'm not promising that I'll take yours; I promised that I'll listen to what you have to say and decide after."

"Sounds good."

"Now are you the same Doc that I continue to hear about in Balad?"

"You mean, for these charges."

"No, I was told by a soldier in my unit that if I fly out to Balad, I should look up a man they call Doc."

"Are you kidding?"

"No, apparently you orchestrated a mission that allowed one of her friends to sleep there and then threw a party or something."

"Yeah, I guess that's me."

"Really, because of you, Balad has become like a vacation spot."

"Well, as you can imagine I've been out of that game for some time now, but I'm sure my guys are doing all they can to help out your guys."

"Well, it's a pleasure to meet you."

"Thank you."

"Alright, for the charges pending. You're accused of stealing some guns and trying to sell them to the Iraqis."

"What?"

"From the Rat's statement, he said that you told him to bring them to a contractor camp where he thought you were going to try to trade them to the Iraqis."

This shit just got a lot more serious. I felt sick to my stomach. I realized that, although I wasn't taking it easy, I definitely wasn't taking it hard enough. High treason was punishable by death. I had signed a paper that started with my name and ended with punishable by death? Self-preservation, that's what time it was. I disobeyed Arilious' orders and told him the whole story. I told him everything, and like Arilious said, he moved to plea bargain. He read me the charges I was charged with and the maximum punishment for each; that's called trumped-up charges and is usually used by law enforcement, not by lawyers. When all was said and done, I was looking at one hundred and some odd years. He then asked me about my family. He said, "We'll need them for sympathy." I was twenty-one years old; this was my problem, not my family's. They were not going to be dragged into this. And as for sympathy, if I wanted sympathy, I would have committed suicide. He said that I wasn't doing all I could do to save my own ass, and I told him that would be his job. I stood up and grabbed a nonalcoholic beer out of his little refrigerator.

"What are you doing?"

"Oh, I'm sorry. Do you mind if I have a drink?"

He started to laugh.

"I'll take the case."

He had told me to write down everything I had told him then sign the statement. I wrote down the story but refused to sign it. I took heed of what Arilious had told me; I couldn't let anyone get their hands on a signed confession, not even my lawyer. He explained that if this went to a high-treason accusation, he would need all he could get as soon as he could get it. I put my trust in the fact that Arilious knew what he was talking about and didn't sign the statement.

Arilious was waiting for me when I made it out of the office to reassure me that I had done the right thing.

"Do not trust anyone but me."

I would follow that statement to the T. During our walk back, I began to humanize myself to Sexy and Hottie. I began talking as if we were old friends after a long absence. We spent the time talking about our parents, our siblings, our favorite vacation spots, love, and life. I found them tarnished and hardened from the regular Army. Their education was the military, and they never questioned it. They found me as a man instead of a soldier; before I would listen to anyone, they would have to prove themselves to me, not to Uncle Sam. I questioned every order and didn't follow it if I felt it was wrong, stupid, or if I was hungover that day. It's easy to say that they had never met anyone like me, and their curiosity would come to get the best of them.

The flight back to Balad was short and upon exiting the Black Hawk Arilious and I began to walk slowly back to the company area. Before we could give each other a departing hand shake, we were interrupted by the word Topp became famous for screaming.

"Doc!"

Before I was brought under federal indictment Topp would utilize me as his watchdog. He knew my hatred ran deep for most of the men there and when people crossed him I was his tool of revenge. From acquiring sensitive items to halting the increasing traffic in front of his office, if he wanted to make the officer's lives harder I was only a shout away. As he approached, Arilious quickly fell back so as not to interrupt whatever mission Topp had in store.

"Who is it this time Topp?"

Without saying a word he walked right past. Before I could make up the pace he was already standing at the picnic table we so frequently used to plot our revenge. I can't remember the conversation verbatim, so I'll sum it up. Topp had just returned from a meeting with the Sgt. Maj. and the section leaders, in this meeting Sgt. Maj. revealed his plan to convoy back through Iraq in one months' time. Even with C-130 airplanes waiting to fly the entire unit over the battle ground, Sgt. Maj. decided the unit would drive. The problem was that with available cargo room on the C-130's even the higher ups back in the states didn't understand why Sgt. Maj. would be risking the lives of soldiers in a convoy. So unless the convoy was made up of one hundred percent volunteers, the generals back home were most likely going to rule against. Topp continued on to say that the section leaders not only refused, but wouldn't even volunteer any of their subordinates.

"Good, it's about time they stand up against that asshole."

"Hold on Doc, I'm not finished yet."

As he continued his frustration became apparent. He kicked his leg up and placed his boot on the seat of the bench, his arms folded and resting on his elevated knee. He paused for short while, and then regained his composure.

"Doc, I told the Sgt.Maj. that there was only one person in this unit that was crazy enough to volunteer."

Apparently, here's where I came in. I couldn't believe what I was hearing. Their plan was for me to volunteer, and with me the rest of the VLA. Once; or if we made it to Kuwait, military police would re-arrest me and fly me back to Balad for trial. They actually thought that when their ranking sergeants failed to put their soldier's lives on the line for the Sgt. Major's ego, that they could come to me and I would use my VLA rank to put my soldier's lives on the line. This piece of shit Sgt Maj. thought that he would lead the men he fucked over the worst, and failed to represent into battle, and then to use me as a pawn to do it. An hour before, this motherfucker was trying to send me to jail for a hundred years, now he wants me to help. To be honest I thought it a little ironic. They've worked so hard to diminish our group, canceled Louisiana Saturday Nights, sent in spy's to find out what we were planning, even isolated me from everyone else, and now, when they need real soldiers, they come to us.

"Sorry Topp, I can't help you."

"Then you should know, Doc, I won't feel safe out there without you."

Checkmate. The Sgt. Maj. used Topp as a pawn. He knew that I wouldn't let Topp go alone. That son of a bitch had me in a corner.

"Alright Topp, I'll do it. Let me talk to the guys."

Before the conversation ended I noticed Sgt. Maj. peering at us from the porch of the HQ building. He quickly called Topp and they disappeared around the corner. When Topp reemerged he informed me to keep all of this quite until the final decision was made. The truth is I never heard another word about it. Maybe the Sgt. Maj. couldn't handle the thought of coming to me for help, I'm not sure, but whatever it was, I'm thankful now. I don't believe that I've told anybody about that until now. So I would like to add that Topp's volunteering was done through his honor and courage. Topp you're an amazing leader and a man I would declare war for any day. And to the men of the VLA, you motherfuckers were storm troopers. If anything is to be remembered from this book it's that they came to us when the war intruded on their mission to attain awards.

That night back at my confinements, I decided to take a stroll. I hadn't been outside without an escort in a month, and since mine were both in the bathroom, I figured now was as good a time as any. I made my way to Arilious and talked to him for a second. He informed me that the plan to turn Hottie and Sexy was in full swing. When the prosecutor asked them what they thought of me, they had told him, "You're going to have a hard time putting him away." He also told me that they invited me over to their room for board games, but I would have to sneak in. I then returned to the old stomping grounds of Mo-town. I sat down and had a drink with most of the guys, who were eager to hear what was going on with me. Giff brought me up-to-date on the black ops.

"Everyone's taking care of themselves; we go to the Nepali camp and just pick up enough for ourselves. No one is really selling it anymore."

All the better; I had other shit on my mind.

I then decided to swing by and check out Moto and the Hawaiians. Their flights had not been cancelled as ours had, and they had been making regular trips to Baghdad. Although Moto was a main distributor, he also had a big mouth. He informed most of his unit where and how to get it. Soon, he was one of many distributors. I decided to help him out. I told him I'd try to set up a meeting between him and the Nepalese. I told him it would be soon but I didn't give an expected date. I had been gone about two hours now and thought it would be best to return. As I walked through Mo-town on my way to my confinements, I heard a voice.

"Son of a bitch, come with me."When I turned around, it was Sgt. Fish.

"How you doin', Sgt. Fish?"

"Shut up, and come with me."

As we walked, I tried to make small talk with only silence in return. He was pissed, and he had every right to be. When he opened the door, Sgt. Stress was pacing back and forth like his daughter was on a date with Knight Ryder.

"Gents, how's it hanging?"

"Don't start your cute little bullshit with us. We are supposed to watch you twenty-four hours a day, and the moment we give you a little trust, you disappear. From now on, no more trust. From now on, one of us will go everywhere you go."

"I'm sorry, fellows, to my understanding you two are supposed to follow *me*. I'm not restricted from going anywhere; you just have to follow me when I go. So you fucked up, and now you're blaming it on me."

"You're right; we are supposed to follow you. But what if I went to tell Chip that you snuck away from us to get drunk? Then maybe he would change the rules a little bit, maybe put the noose a little tighter."

"Sure, you can do that. Then I would be forced to inform him about the excessive drinking that goes on in here. Not to mention wine making and sexual relationships with soldiers under direct chain of command."

Check, check mate. They stood in disbelief. They couldn't understand how a man who did what I did could even threaten them with snitching. I was the biggest criminal out there, and I was threatening them on a little drinking. The room was silent for an agonizing thirty seconds.

"Is that how you want to play? That's fine. Sgt. Fish and I are on opposite twelve-hour shifts; you will join him for his twelve hours on, and when he gets off, you will come with me for my twelve hours on."

It was a beautiful plan. I didn't believe they came up with it themselves. It included everything that pissed me off: twenty-four hour observation, keeping me in the open for any old asshole to pick me for a detail, and sleep deprivation. Sgt. Stress was a genius, but I think he had underestimated me. I went through the next couple days with very little sleep while I was being handed around like a cigarette in prison. Sweeping, packing, helping people get ready for the long travel home, anyone who mentioned a task, Sgt. Stress was happy to hand me out. When night fell, I would then tell Sgt. Fish the day's happenings. Sgt. Stress would also try to share my free labor throughout the night. Officers showed up at Sgt. Fish's place of work at all hours, trying to get me to help them with whatever bullshit they had going on. Sgt. Fish always had the same response.

"I don't care what Sgt. Stress said, right now he's in my charge, and I said no."

There was the chink in the armor. Though I knew about the fight they had had, I thought all was good, but obviously I was still in the middle of a power struggle. Sgt. Fish had won the fistfight, but in the Army that was by no means the end all. Sgt. Stress was still higher in rank. So, as Sgt. Stress was busy trying to fuck me, Sgt. Fish was helping me by constantly trying to fuck Sgt. Stress. I knew that if I wanted this twenty-four hour bullshit to end, I would have to exploit this hatred.

Soon, I was constantly complaining to Sgt. Fish about the unfair treatment I was receiving from Sgt. Stress. At the expense of sounding like a bitch, I had both of them working harder and harder to undermine each other. It finally came to a head when

Sgt. Fish and I were released early and the three of us had to be in the same room for a whole night. With a display of true insubordination, Sgt. Fish asked if I would like a drink right in front of Sgt. Stress.

"I'm going to have to put my foot down. You're fucking up by trusting the little prick, Sgt. Fish."

Sgt. Fish realized that he was right and couldn't leave himself unguarded. As he paused, I figured if he was unsure now, he wouldn't be if he had a couple of drinks in him. I'd drunk with him before, and I knew he was one carefree son of a bitch on the devil's nectar.

"He's right, Sgt. Fish, but you should have a couple. Hell, what's it been, a week?"

"Yeah, I'm gonna have a couple."

Sgt. Stress would once again help me with that gaping hole in his head. "Well, don't do it here. If you have to drink, you need to go far away from me."

Sgt. Fish rolled his eyes, shook his head, and walked out the door. At the time I thought it had backfired. I lay in my cot and chose sleep rather than sharing conversation with Sgt. Stress.

Later that night, I was awakened by someone tugging at my foot.

"Sssssssshhhhhhh, it's Fish."

"What's up, Sgt. Fish?"

"Come on, come have a couple of drinks with the guys."

Busted. Sgt. Stress was expecting a night attack and was on his feet before I could put my feet on the ground.

"No, he's not going anywhere. They could fuck me if he gets caught drinking, and if he leaves, I'm going talk to Topp!"

"Shut the fuck up, Stress. I'll drag you outside and wear you out again."

With that, Sgt. Stress was out the door to somewhere, and Fish realized the severity of it all. He jumped in bed, and I did my best to act like I was asleep until I really was. The next morning, Sgt. Stress came in to pack up his shit. He was leaving, moving to the HQ; apparently living under these conditions was too stressful. I couldn't say that I was sad to see him go, but I thought that, without him, they would be keeping a closer eye on me. I should have realized that with the main party leaving in a week, they could care less about me.

Everyone was so wrapped up in packing and trying to smuggle war memorabilia home that I was left to run amok. Over the next couple of weeks, I began a less than professional relationship with Sgt. Hottie. I knew what the prosecutor was doing before he did. All along, he was so tight on evidence, his best move would have been an acquittal. He made a move at the Nepali crew, who didn't say a word. He threatened them with everything from sending them home to jail time, and yet they held their ground. I couldn't say if it was their undying loyalty to me or the talk Arilious had with them an hour before their interrogation. His next move was to retrieve the piece of weapon that we couldn't find in the DFAC pit. He knew that if he put my unit up to the task, I would probably end up with the part myself. Instead, he forced men from two other units to climb through the pit from sunrise to sunset. They should have wanted my blood for that, but to my surprise, I had the piece in hand before midnight. They would have had to fly in a unit from Kuwait if they were really serious about getting that piece. He had nothing; he was getting desperate, and I was getting a good laugh every night. Sgt. Hottie finally informed me that they were going to begin offering deals to the two White Devils, deals that they probably wouldn't be able to pass up. This would be the first time that I could be blamed for being naïve.

"Don't worry about them; I have them under control."

Since every person left in my unit was out-processing from their jobs, they usually only worked for about an hour in the morning. They would go to the morning briefing, make sure the new Active Army unit was off to a good start, and then leave to continue packing and preparing. After the packing was done, there were a lot of soldiers with a lot of free time on their hands, including Sgt. Fish and me. My confinements once again became the place to be. Instead of intense parties that lasted throughout the night, the parties instead lasted through the whole day with an hour or two in the middle to pass out or do the dirty deed. The day before the main party was supposed to leave, during one of these parties, Arilious showed up with a very distraught look on his face.

"Doc, can we get some privacy?"

Without me saying a word, Sgt. Fish jumped up and cleared the room of everyone.

"Arilious, this doesn't look like it's going to make me happy."

"Do you want to sit down?"

"You watch too many movies; get on with it."

"Both of the White Devils are going to plea bargain. They don't want them anymore; now they're using all of their capabilities to put you behind bars."

He was right, I should've sat down. My legs got weak, and I fell to the bed. For the first time, I was at a loss for words. I just sat there with my head in my hands.

"Doc, what do you want us to do?"

I guess he noticed the confusion on my face when I looked up at him. I heard him loud and clear when he nodded his head up and down. I knew he would have done it; I knew whoever he meant when he said "us" would have done it. It was check, check mate. I never in a million years thought I would be capable of giving that order, but now I know what people feel like when they're put in a corner.

"Arilious, I need to see the chaplain."

"You don't get it; this shit just got real. I thought at first that you might get out of this, but now..."

"Just get the chaplain."

"Why? You don't even believe in God."

"What I believe in is very questionable right now. Not believing in him hasn't helped me thus far, and now you're asking me to..."

"I'm not asking you to do anything. What I'm saying is that you can't talk your way out of this anymore. And right now, I definitely don't need you crying to a priest. The chaplain might be a priest or whatever, but he's still a soldier. Do not trust anyone, god damn it."

"What are the assistants saying?"

"They just gave me the news. Your lawyer doesn't know yet; therefore, you don't know yet."

"I feel beaten. I don't know what to do. Just give me a night to think about it."

"I understand...but there's something else. They want me as far away from this as possible. I'm ordered to leave tomorrow with the main body. Tonight is my last night. I leave in the morning."

This day was a punch in the nuts for everyone. Working in the hospital, Hollie's infidelities, it was all nothing compared to this day. For some reason after he left, I became upset with him. I thought he had finally turned his back on me and left me to get ripped apart. I worked myself up until I had finished a bottle and a half. I shouldn't have been awake, much less walking around searching for Sgt. Hottie and Spc. Sexy. I went to their rooms without a bit of subtlety. I banged on their doors, asked their friends for their location, and at one point just sat on Sgt. Hottie's doorstep. This is where a 35ish black female sergeant found me. She took me into her room and gave me a juice. The conversation that followed is very vague in my memory, but I do remember tearing up. A woman I had never met before that night and didn't remember the next day had finally broken me. We talked, we prayed, and the truth is that that was the night that the Lord finally found me in the darkness, like I was that sock behind the dryer. I owe that woman a lot and will probably never be able to repay her, but if she reads this, I would just like to say, "Whether I make it to heaven or go straight to hell, I will sing your praises when I get there."

I slept deeper than I've ever slept that night, and when I awoke, I thought the whole thing had been a nightmare. It's a beautiful moment, right when you wake up from a nightmare and realize that all that had happened was torment that you had put on yourself. When I looked at the clock and realized I had missed lunch, I wasn't even a bit upset, because behind my clock was the most beautiful group of people I had ever seen. Arilious, Sgt. Hottie, and Spc. Sexy were all sitting at the edge of my bed. I started laughing.

"I had the craziest fucking dream."

"Doc, I heard what happened last night."

"Oh shit, it wasn't a dream," I said, putting my hands over my face.

Spc. Sexy spoke up, looking pissed off with her arms folded. "Last night or everything."

Then Arilious said, "It doesn't matter; none of it's a dream."

"Then why are you still here?"

"Apparently, if you were looking for an angel, I'm here. Last night, while you were trying to ruin everything we've worked for, I was getting clearance to stay with you until this thing is over."

"Who would approve that?"

"We know too much. I assured them that no one would be dragged into this if it went downhill. No reach for public attention or writing of a *tell all* book."

"Yeah, yeah, that could be done."

"The only way to get a fair trial is to get you back to the States."

"What do you suggest?"

"Get a lawyer on it from the other side, see if they might arrange the trial to be held there."

"OK."

Chapter Seventeen

Put the Women and Children to Bed

Arilious went to find the White Devils while I made my way to the Internet tent to see if my lawyer had found out the bad news. Opening up his negative e-mails were always the low part of my day. On this particular day, I was in no mood to hear his shit. His bargains had gone from five years, to three years, and on the last e-mail was down to one year in prison. Today, they had pulled all bargains; they wanted me to go to trial with three men against me. My lawyer informed me that he was going to request the five-year bargain again and hope they took it. My rebuttal was simple: "You're either for me or against me, and I am no longer going to bargain. If they want me, then they have their work cut out for them." I had a new hope, God and Arilious were now on my side, and those two are all a man needs. Later that evening, it was his turn to rebut. He claimed that he had only taken this case because he thought I would be smart enough to plea out. He said he didn't have time to go through long, drawn-out court proceedings and that he'd recommend other lawyers in Iraq. He was the best, and he was running with his tail between his legs.

The main body was gone, and there were only a few people left from my unit, mostly pilots and flight ops. That night, I found myself with most of the pilots. They had piled into my room to hear firsthand all the shit that I was capable of. We drank, and they laughed, and I gained more friends that night, one of whom would become my company commander.

Capt. Lui: mid 30s, 5'9" - VLA Status: Honorary. Morals: High. Capt. Lui ate a lot of shit when he was a lieutenant under a real prick of a commander. He was in touch with the little soldier and was loved by the VLA. He was a good man, and it was a cause for celebration when he snatched the commander position away from Chip.

We told stories until morning time, and yet Sgt. Fish wasn't back yet. When the room cleared out, I decided to take a walk and find my escort. I was so caught up with talking to the officers, I didn't realize that what was left of the VLA was partying in Giff's room. I received salutes as I walked into the door. Everyone by that time was extremely inebriated and was just sort of lying around. As we started an extra inning of bullshit, another bottle was opened. It started getting deep when everyone was silenced with a *wap* sound. When I turned around, I saw Sgt. Fish with his head turned and a younger female soldier jumping up from his lap. Apparently, she had given him a titty twister, and when he returned the favor she slapped him. He could barely walk, but I decided that now was probably the best time to get him to bed. I threw him over my shoulder and began my short walk. Once we made it to our front steps, I set him down for some reason, maybe to open the door, I forget, but when I did, he fell off the steps and scraped both his wrists. We laughed, and I threw him into bed. I made my way back to make sure that this would stay between the VLA, and then I returned to my room.

When I returned to the room, the door was already open, and when I looked inside, Sgt. LT. was standing over Sgt. Fish.

"Doc, what happened here?"

"I don't know. I just went to the bathroom."

She started yelling at Sgt. Fish, something about going to breakfast with her, and then she whipped the sheets right off of him.

"Oh, my God, Doc, did he take pills or something?"

"I don't think so. Why?"

"Oh, my God, I'm going get the doctor. I think he tried to cut his wrists."

With the joke being over, she ran out of the room. I quickly jumped up to check the scrapes; they were still just scrapes. I collected all of the bottles, empty or full, and made my way to Giff's room. I didn't even have time to explain when I threw a dozen or so bottles into his door. I ran back to my room, but by that time, it was too late. Sgt. LT. and Chip had lifted Sgt. Fish up and had begun making their way out of the room. Chip just couldn't keep his mouth shut as he walked by me.

"For some reason, you're always in the wrong place."

Still out of breath, I couldn't say a word. I just shook my head in regret. Somehow, this prick was going blame this shit on me.

It wasn't long before I was called to the HQ for a one-on-one with Chip. Apparently, when Sgt. Fish reported to the HQ, he thought it easier to tell them it was an attempted suicide, rather than explain the real story. If he had told the truth, he probably would have lost rank or worse. Instead, a tiny fib rewarded him with medication and a trip on the next thing smoking towards Kuwait. He did the smart thing. On the other hand, I was out another escort and was going to be forced with someone for the next week that they were in country. Chip blamed me for the added stress that caused Sgt. Fish's fake suicide and had me report to Sgt. Waterfalls.

Sgt. Waterfalls: mid 20s, 6'0" - VLA Status: Member. Morals: High. Waterfalls and I got along well. Like so many other soldiers, both of us had cheating girlfriends, but unlike me he would not exact revenge no matter how hard I tried. He talked about his ex constantly and was quite broken up about it, but I enjoyed him; he reminded me what real human beings were like.

Waterfalls' room was vacant of everything. He had nothing but two beds and the same number of lockers. During the day, he had no task but to escort me to the computer tent to write my lawyer, but even that took a backseat to his constant weight lifting. He allowed me to do as I wished by myself as long as I was back in the room at night. I decided to take this time to contact my family and Hollie. I told my family that everything was fine and I'd be home soon, but I told Hollie that I had changed for the worst. I told her I wasn't the same man I was when I left and that it would be best if she moved on, because I didn't know if I was coming home. Even if I did make it home I told her, she would only get maybe two good years out of me before I had a mental breakdown or worst. I remember her response: "You don't expect me to wait forever, do you?" Fuck, Hollie, you couldn't wait three months. I can't expect anything, especially with someone reminding constantly what I shouldn't expect. No, I didn't say that, but I sure thought it. My family was taken care of; now it was time for me.

I hadn't contacted my lawyer since our last e-mail, and I decided not to until I tied up a few loose strings on my side. While Sgt. Hottie informed me daily that no new evidence was found, Arilious pressured me to do something about the White Devils' statements.

"It's the only thing the prosecutor has; without it, he admits he doesn't have a case. It's the only way you'll be acquitted."

I wasn't a fool. I knew I had to make a move, but with my court date nowhere in sight, I figured I had a little time. The next day brought the departure of the rest of my unit, including my escort. The only people to stay were Chip, Sgt. Stress, and I thought Arilious, but that day also brought bad news. There was no one there left on our side to authorize Arilious' stay. He was to be gone with the rest, but ten minutes before his flight, he continued to do his job. With a phone call from across base, and the last time Arilious and I would ever talk, he let me know that my court date was set a month from that day.

That day also brought something that I didn't understand, something consistently standardized, something without reason or remorse, without equality or freedom, something that I hadn't seen since boot camp. I was handed off to an Active Army unit, the same Active Army unit that had taken my unit's place, and the same Active Army unit that was briefed on all situations far and wide by none other than Chip himself. They treated me like the piece of shit soldier I had become. I wasn't the charming, handsome misguided young man that my unit knew me to be, because they wouldn't take the time to get to know me. They stuck me with a young specialist who took his job way too seriously. I mean, obviously he wasn't that important to the cause; they made him babysit me, but if babysitting was his mission, then he was going to try to get an award for it. I found it funny, but apparently everyone didn't have my same sense of humor.

With time beating down on me, I had to do something to get in touch with the White Devils, but with my new escort, it would be next to impossible. I had no messengers, and Sexy and Hottie were weary of coming around me with my new shadow. I hatched a plan to get in touch with Moto through our MySpace code.

MySpace code: With military surveillance covering phones, computers, and any letters addressed to suspicious locations, the soldiers in Iraq were forced to come up with a secure way to communicate. MySpace.com was a site to promote your best pictures, qualities, and attributes to the community in hopes of finding people who are like you or maybe even someone who will fall in love with you for your marketing abilities and your use of graphics/songs that define you, and it was also used more appropriately for covert ops. Anything sent through the computer could be read by military intel, but anything that was saved as a default on your page wasn't sent anywhere at all; therefore, it wasn't read. Although it was there on your page for anyone to see, we highly doubted the people that mattered were checking our MySpace pages. Here's an example of one of our MySpace page info boards.

Heroes: Gen. North, Gen. Gates.

Books: 2300, w/2 pair, 4 to 6 kids. Bring it.

Hobbies: Hanging out at Mo-town.

Sports: Anything with Big Vin.

Message: Go to the North Gate at 11:00 p.m. with two pair of shoes, sizes four and six kids. Bring whatever is given to you there to Mo-town and give it to Big Vin.

All that was left was for the right person to check your page, and since we hadn't used the code in so long, I doubted Moto was going to my page for anything.

Although I didn't think it would work, I figured it was worth a shot. As I waited for my escort to come out of their newly attained HQ, which I was so familiar with, I noticed a large black man walking at me with a purpose. As he cut his shoulder and walked past me, I felt it appropriate to show him that I was peaceful and to hopefully avoid another scare from happening later, so I started with my Southern charm.

"What's going down, big dog."

Before I knew it, his face was two inches away from mine. "What did you just say to me?"

"I said, what's going down."

At the top of his lungs now, he shouted, "Who am I?"

"Who are you?"

"Yes, soldier, who am I?"

Shaking my head in confusion, I said, "Sorry, I got nothing."

"Am I not a sergeant major!"

"That's right, you are; I'm sorry."

Then he just paused and stared at me as if I were naked. "Then why...are you...not...in parade rest when you are talking to me!"

"Oh, I forgot about the old parade rest; it's been so long." I smiled and shook it off and then apologized. Apparently, even when you apologize, you have to be in parade rest. In the moment before he exploded, a female stepped out of the HQ to take a look at was what was going on.

"Sgt. Major, this is one of the remaining soldiers from the last unit that we were briefed on."

"Then, First Sergeant, you'd better get him out of my area of operations before something bad happens."

"Doc, can you come to my office please? Thank you, Sgt. Major."

Maybe my luck was about to change. A female first sergeant. I've never met a female superior who could be harsh with me; maybe it's my boyish good looks or my Southern accent. I don't know, but what I do know is that she was very understanding, even to me.

"Doc, I understand your malcontent with this man's Army. I don't expect you to be respectful to whom you believe to be the enemies. I've heard a lot about you, and I fear the corruption of my unit; you know it only takes one bad apple. After seeing your delicate handling of the Sgt. Major, I've decided to keep you away from here. I'm sure you'd prefer that."

"I would."

"There's a man who extended his stay from the last tour. All he's waiting for is the paperwork to be approved back in the States, and then he'll be shipped to Baghdad. I'm guessing that will probably take longer than your stay here. He's your new escort, and neither of you are allowed in our area of operation. I'll have my man take you to him right now."

Damn, another escort and another room; this was starting to get tiresome. Has anyone been counting rooms? As my escort walked me back to the trailer area, he was laying his last bit of authority down on deaf ears.

"You're going to behave. You're not going to give this soldier a hard time. What he says goes." Yada fuckin' yada.

Finally, we made it to the door of the trailer. He knocked with the same intensity he had with everyday life. A larger-than-life fellow answered. I stared him straight in the eyes and shook my head with a silent no.

"Soldier, if we could step inside, I have to brief you on your next mission."

Then he flung his head around to me. "You don't move."

I waited outside the door for maybe two minutes, and then it was flung open again. As my old escort stepped down the steps, the large fellow made sure I knew who was in charge.

"This is your new home; get in here."

I tipped my head to my previous escort and stepped inside the empty room. When the door closed behind me, I turned around to look my new captor in the eyes. He threw his arms wide, and I came in for the hug. It was Tank.

Tank: mid 20s, 6'3 - VLA Status: Member. Morals: Medium Low. Tank joined our unit in Kuwait and had been a personal friend ever since. He flew with communications constantly, and I hadn't spoken to him in months. He was put in the group with Big Vin and Deffes of the men I would much rather have on my side than the other.

We broke apart laughing, and I said, "Did you let on that you knew me?"

"No, I saw you shake your head."

"Good."

"Everyone told me that you were in jail."

"Was, but not anymore."

"Well, the way your escort made it sound, if I wasn't careful, you'd kill me while I slept."

"That's why he was always so intense, he was scared. No, you know better than that; c'mon, where the hell would I hide a body as big as yours?"

We both smiled.

"Listen, Tank, I don't want you to get in trouble, but I have a lot of things to take care of."

"Fuck them, you're the boss."

"Alright, if anyone asks..."

"If anyone asks, I'll tell them to get bent."

"Tank, I don't have the words."

"For once, really?" He smiled. "Just get out of here."

My first move was to get to the phone and contact my eldest sister. She was hooked up with anyone who was anyone. Lawyers, judges, congressman, senators, they all knew Valeris by first name. I told her the story exactly how I told it here and told her to run amok in the new world. The next thing was the White Devils. I found them both in the same place and explained why it would be best for them to forget my name. They weren't happy, but they understood. They told me that their court date was a day before mine, so the fact of the matter was I wouldn't know what they said in court until the day before I went to trial. It wasn't a very big window, but I contacted my lawyer with the verdict. We don't make a move until they go to trial. He thought I was nuts, and again he tried to pass me off to another lawyer, but I never contacted him back for his plan to go through. In one day, I had gotten a ball rolling. I didn't know which way it was rolling, but it was rolling.

That night, I went to the Hawaiians for a place to sleep. From what I understood, over the last five months, Moto has taken my directive and turned his unit into a cash cow. Although he handled everything personally, which wasn't my style, he did seem to get respect. He had taken the craps table and turned it into a thriving casino with amenities including alcohol and smoke. His fist may not have been iron, but in a unit that was that laid back it didn't have to be. Well, maybe he was a little soft with certain people, but it seemed to be working for him. That night though, Moto's soft side took a back seat to the heat that was on me. He met me outside with some distressing news. The Hawaiian command had banned me from being over there, and anyone who was caught with me would be punished. I guess there's no gratitude among criminals. Yeah, I guess I helped make him the godfather of his unit, probably put more cash in his pocket than was in my own, but I was too hot, and he couldn't take the chance of being seen with me. Another door closed in my face. Not to say that I blame Moto at all. It showed that he, unlike me, understood the term "laying low" and from what I hear he became a greater Godfather than I ever was.

While I was leaving the Hawaiian trailer area, I heard a recognizable voice in the distance. As the shadow got closer, I realized it was the guy who had tried to steal my alcohol.

"Doc, can you come check something out for me?"

"I'm not a medic anymore. Go to sick call in the morning."

"If I was hurt, I'd need a medic, but I need you, get the picture?"

We made our way to his room, and spread out on his bed were five compact pistols.

"They're the pistols 007 uses. I taxed them from a flight headed to Fallujah."

"This isn't regular military issue. Whoever these are for will be looking for them."

"No, there were like a hundred of them; they'll never notice. Look, we need someone who knows how to handle things like this. We'd like to get them home."

"You could get good money for these. Stolen military guns are expensive on the streets because they can't be led back to anyone. That's your lesson for today; good luck getting them home."

"Doc, please, we need your help getting them home. There's no one else who could do this shit."

I couldn't help but laugh. "This is a setup. My advice is take them back to their rightful owners."

"I swear it's not a setup."

I opened the door and walked out; he followed.

"Leave your blouse inside," I said without turning.

We walked a good distance away from the trailer, and I patted down his chest. Out there, it was unlikely for the prosecutor to get a wire, but better safe than sorry. I figured if there was a recorder it was somewhere in the room, so I threw him a bone.

"Open up your television set and tape them securely inside, around wires, make them look like part of the TV."

"But can't dogs smell guns?"

"These guns probably haven't been shot yet, but even if they have, it doesn't matter. Anything too big to travel with is going by ship. There won't be any dogs, just a visual inspection."

He smiled a smile that made me think MPs were going to come out from every direction, but none did. He thanked me and returned to his room. The thrill got me again. I regretted it immediately. It was probably a setup, and even if it wasn't, the thing between me and God had just been broken. I decided to take a stroll to the Nepali camp...and never leave.

Looking at the lights of the base from the Nepali camp took me out of the war completely. It made me say "them" instead of "us." It was as if I was watching the war on television thousands of miles away. I stayed there for three weeks. I thought back on the nomads we had passed first coming into the country, miles away from anything, just trying to survive. But they weren't trying to survive, they were trying to be free. They were caught in a country that could do what they wanted, no matter how unjust, and their only option was to pilgrimage to a place where no one could find them. They were living hard by our standards, but they were free from false persecution. They were free from a monarchy, they were free from everything. There wasn't a soul there to help, only hurt, so why not go somewhere where you can only depend on yourself? I understood the mindset of the nomads. I was a nomad.

I hadn't seen another soldier in two weeks, and I can't say I was depressed about it. I ate, slept, showered, and socialized with the Nepali only. We drank and laughed until our stomachs hurt every night. On this particular night, I decided to go to the Internet tent for my 2:00 a.m. e-mail check, but before I made it out of the Nepali gate, I was confronted by a chubby master sergeant whom I'd never seen before.

"Excuse me, soldier."

"You're excused."

"Hey, don't walk away from me. Who are you? Why are you over here, and where the hell is your rank?"

"Me...I'm Doc. I live here, and I don't have any."

"Oh, I'm sorry, are you a soldier?"

"I used to be."

He got louder. "I don't have time for this. Who's your commander?"

"I don't have one."

He started breathing heavily. "Come with me. We're going to get this shit straight."

"Master Sergeant, no disrespect, but if you don't know me, you'd better ask somebody before you start barking orders."

"Excuse me, soldier!"

"I told you, you're excused."

"Who are you?" he said, like I had just flown there in leotards and a cape.

"If you're going to keep asking the same questions, then let me lay it out for you. If you want my rank, you'll have to go back about six months; if you want my commander, you'll have to go to Kuwait, and if you want me to leave, well then, I'm leaving."

He was taken aback for a second. "AAAhhhh...Alright, well I'm in charge of everything inside of the Nepali camp, and I heard that there's some soldier back here fucking around."

"If I see any, I'll let you know."

"OK, yeah, well thank you."

The son of a bitch thanked me before I left, can you believe it? Thank God he did, because I only had a day left before my trial, and I didn't need any more publicity.

Valeris' e-mail had nothing good, and the White Devils' trial was the next day. I didn't feel real good. Maybe I should have taken a day away from the Nepalis to talk to them more recently. Of course, they understood when I was standing right in front of them, but it had almost been a month since I had a sit-down with them. They had signed statements that they would have to back out on, not including the pressure that was being put on them by their lawyers. I had no doubt that they were going to hang me, so fuck it, let's get drunk.

Lunch was approaching by the time I woke up the next morning. I made up my mind. I'd go and get a fresh uniform, take a hot shower, eat a good lunch, contact my lawyer, and ten years of imprisonment, here I come. I made it to Tank's room in record time in fear of missing lunch. When I opened the door, he laughed.

"Where the hell have you been? I thought you had already left."

"Has someone been looking for me?"

"Yeah right, who else would worry about you but me?"

I closed the door behind me and sat on the bed for a short good-bye speech. I don't think he cared, but he was the only one I could tell it to. In the middle of the wordy, overly emotional exchange, the next room broke into a ruckus. As I tried to continue, I heard the neighbor's door slam, and then it was our turn. Someone who was excited was at the door. Tank jumped up to answer it.

"Doc, you need to pack up everything you own; your flight leaves in thirty minutes."

The man at the door was looking directly at Tank. Tank turned to me, and we started to laugh. I stood up and threw my arms around Tank.

"Well, this is it. If you're ever swinging through Baghdad..."

"Doc, we need to be across base in thirty minutes. Please hurry," the man at the door objected.

"Look, buddy, I'm in no rush to go to prison, so you..."

"Prison? Doc you're going home. The two other men testified that you had nothing to do with it."

I doubt I can explain in words, but I'll try. I felt it once before when I slipped a kiss in on a young girl who I fancied. The moment I realized that she was kissing me back was the same feeling. It was the feeling of going about something all wrong but it still turning out in your favor. I couldn't stand, I couldn't talk, and once again my face made it to my hands. I sure am crying a lot in this book, but please don't take me as a pussy. I was just in a stressful situation. Tank packed up everything I owned and put it by the door. He picked me up to my feet, and the last words we ever shared were, "Don't worry, I won't tell anyone that you're a little bitch."

I just laughed and was led out by the guy at the door.

Chapter Eighteen

What Kind of Party Is It When
I Jump out of the Cake

The flight was quick, and I was in Kuwait before midnight. The guy who brought me was back on the plane before the next takeoff. This was the first time in five months that I wasn't required to have an escort. There was no one looking for me, and for the first time in a long time, I was under the radar. My unit was the last thing I was looking for when I asked a passerby where to sleep. He told me that usually the people off the flights sleep in a warehouse behind the theater. I found the theater and found the warehouse. I figured I'd pay someone in the morning to print me some orders and sneak on a plane. It could have worked.

The next morning I woke up to a surprise. Sgt. Hottie was beside me. I didn't know if I was dreaming. I sat up and moved her hair out of her eyes. With the emerging smile on her face, I knew I wasn't dreaming, she was really there. I told her to go back to sleep, and I got up for breakfast. The DFAC was crawling with soldiers from my unit, men I hadn't seen in months. Once again, I was famous. My name was on a lot of tongues, and I thought it'd be best to report to my unit, but not before I went back to check on Sgt. Hottie.

It wasn't just Sgt. Hottie, Spc. Sexy had made it down too.

"Someone had to bring the court documents to your unit."

"And it just so happened to be you two?"

"Well..."

I leaned in for a kiss. "How did court go?"

"It was crazy; no one even knew who you were. Finally, the prosecutor stood up and said, "Does anyone know Doc? The guy that was in a tent with you both, he was arrested with you. Does no one know who I'm talking about?' and both of them said no."

"Good, ya'll did good."

They were the greatest. I asked them to hold off on bringing the documents to my unit until the day was spent. We went together to the theater for a show. It was *Gladiator*, and if you must know, yes, I cried at the end, but to justify it I received a good bit of sympathy for it. We went to the mall; that's right, there was a mall, and we shopped in the midst of everyone stopping by to give me hugs and asking for the story. That night, we even went to the disco. We danced, sang, shot darts, and such. I had a great time that night, but that would be one of the last for a while. I reported to my unit around 9:00 p.m. All hell broke loose at 9:01 p.m.

"What the fuck is he doing here?"

"How did this happen?"

"I thought he was in jail?"

"Does this flack vest make me look fat?"

These were all questions that I heard. Well, all except the last one.

Chip had left already, but there were many pricks who jumped in his place. I had an escort on me before 9:05 p.m., and I was really hoping to spend the night with Sgt. Hottie. My night was shot; hell, my next three days were shot. To make things worse, Fitz Gerald was there as my liaison to the unit.

"I don't know if you heard, but when we thought we'd never see you again you were replaced as the leader of the VLA."

"Hell, Fitz Gerald, I didn't know there still was a VLA."

"Yeah, right."

"Who was the leader of this *coup d'Ètat?*"

"It wasn't a *coup d'Ètat.* Jagermiester took it from you outright."

"How?"

"Apparently, when the plane landed in the States, he was so drunk he pissed in formation while Chip was talking."

We both laughed. "Then he deserves it. Hail to the king."

He also quietly informed me that they weren't going to let this go down as easily as it seemed. He didn't know what, but he knew they were planning something.

I spent my next three days sober, with Waterfalls at my side, mostly spending time with Sgt. Hottie and Spc. Sexy. I did happen to call my lawyer, though. I needed to fire him so that, if I needed,

I could get another lawyer in the States. During the conversation he sounded nervous.

"I just wanted to say thank you, and I hope everything goes well for you."

"Well, Doc, I'm not sure what happened, but I'm sorry for doubting you."

"I began to doubt myself. Don't worry about it."

"Well, I just hope everything's good between us."

"It is. Not a problem; don't worry."

"Well, it was an honor, and I'm sure that however you did this, you'll do it again and be free and clear."

"Well, that's not your problem anymore, sir. Stay safe."

He had doubts. *He* had doubts. Are you kidding? I was expecting to be in jail for a decade. I didn't care anymore; it was all over, and I was going home. For the last time I said good-bye to Sgt. Hottie and Spc. Sexy. Spc. Sexy, who was engaged, left me with this: "Thank God you're leaving because I'd probably get in trouble if you stayed."

It was something to think about on the long flight home. If those girls ever read this, I thank you for everything, and if the word devout means that I am loyal for life, then you have a devout follower.

Chapter Nineteen

This One's for You, Chip

Returning home for a regular soldier is probably a blissful occasion. For me it was orchestrated by God himself. I was in Louisiana. I was being bused to Fort Polk, yes, but I was still in Louisiana. I was ready for this nightmare to be over. The next morning I figured I'd wake up a different man, no more anarchy, no more going against the grain, just go with the system. It might have been too late for an apology, but it wasn't too late to redeem myself. The military and my family weren't the only two groups I had to convince. I knew that it would take some convincing of myself. I refused to be that man anymore. When the bus doors squealed apart, so did my plan. Some old familiar faces, military police were there to throw handcuffs on me. That man I recently condemned would have to stick around just a little while longer.

Chip set it up perfectly. I actually was stupid enough to believe I was free, to let hope crawl back in my heart. What a gullible fool. My men just looked, shaking their heads as the MPs threw me in the back of the car, but their sad feeling would quickly diminish as they remembered they were home; there was no room for glum. I stayed silent in the back of the car going through everything that had happened, thinking how that fucking idiot Chip had beat me. When we stopped, the building outside my window didn't look much like a prison. In fact, the people who were walking around it looked happy. I figured it was the nuthouse or maybe just a platoon of soldiers who didn't realize there was a war going on, which would make it a platoon of fools. When the MP opened the door, with one phrase he explained everything: "Welcome to medical hold."

They put me with the broke dicks, men who were either too injured to go to war or bitches who would lie to stay out of the face of danger. Either way, I didn't know what the hell I was doing here. I was approached by a man who had first sergeant rank on his collar.

First Sergeant Fairman: mid 40's, 6'4". Being the First Sergeant of medically incapable soldiers isn't the most prestigious position and he knew it. With his towering height and athletic build I doubt his orders were challenged often. He seemed to be a fair man and in the military that's a lot to ask for.

"Soldier, this is your home until your court date. That soldier standing by my front door, that's your escort. He'll be by your side everywhere you go, and you can only go where we approve you to go, which right now, is in your room."

"Beautiful plan, First Sergeant Fairman."

We began walking towards my escort, and I put my hand out. He shook it nervously and then asked First Sergeant Fairman if he could have a word. They told me to wait while they stepped inside. When he reemerged, I was able to get a good look at him. He was a skinny, elderly man standing at about five foot four. If they thought this little fellow was going to stop me if I decided to leave, they were seriously underestimating me. While First Sergeant Fairman watched, the little man led me up some steps and knocked on a door.

"Is this our room?"

"It's your room."

"I get my own room."

"No, this is your escort's room."

"I thought you were my escort?"

"I was, but my leg is pretty fucked up, and if they think I'm going to stop you from going anywhere, then they're wrong."

That's funny; he and I were on the same level. When the door opened, there stood a taller Hispanic man. He looked all smiles, which usually means goofy, but I knew he would have given me a better fight than the old man. When the old man stepped into the door, he told the Hispanic fellow what was to be done. The Hispanic fellow agreed, but it was obvious he was still confused. The little man leaned in and whispered, "*El un mal hombre. Tener cuidado!*" The Hispanic man shook his head in agreement and closed the door. I stood there, uncomfortable about what to do.

"Which one's mine?"

"Bed? This one here," he said, pointing to the right.

I sat on the couch far enough to one side to welcome him to the other. He followed suit, and before I knew it, he stuck out his hand to introduce himself.

Hilderbrant: mid 30s, 6'1". Hilderbrant was pulled from med school for the war. He had already served in the first Gulf War and was either a little loony or playing the part well. His mental status had him in med hold, but it didn't look like he was "awww shucks" about it.

"So, you were in Iraq? How was it?"

"Hot." There was a moment of silence. "Listen I'm not dangerous; you don't have to be careful. In fact, I don't know why people keep saying that."

"You speak Spanish?"

"Not really, but I do know 'be careful.'"

"Well, these people are under a different impression; they don't think you're a very good guy."

"Oh, I'm not a good guy, but I won't hurt you."

He stared at me for a second. "Thanks."

The broke-dick platoon was run like a regular company, formations morning, noon, and night, accountability, eating together, one big, broke-dick family. A week later, I was starting to get accustomed to the monotonous schedule of broke-dick life. Hell, I started to forget why I was even there. Not only did I not call any of my loved ones, but when I was given a chance to see my newly appointed lawyer, I refused. I was home, and for some lapse in my brain I thought that if I just forgot about it, then it wouldn't be happening. Now, looking back on it, I guess I was losing it, but like always, reality comes hard.

It was the worst mistake they made yet. I didn't know it yet, but I had a beehive behind me, and Valeris was continually throwing rocks at it. One morning, my new prosecuting team called me in for a meeting. They had just received the paperwork from Iraq and were planning to try their luck once again. They forced me to contact my lawyer while I was still in their office. I called Valeris, and she informed me that the only thing they were waiting for was my return, and then they were going to make their move. Well, I was home; it was time for another chess game.

That night, First Sergeant Fairman came by to visit. He told me that I was no longer to be escorted. I was free to do anything I'd like as long as I was in three formations a day. I was given leave on every weekend and could be at the bar every night. Whatever my lawyer threatened them with, it worked. Hell, the truth is that I was never completely told who was on my side. I guess if I were to still go down or decided to write a book, I would be a liability to their governorship or campaign or whatever. I still didn't let my guard down. I figured that, once they declared me a "risk of flight," I'd be donned with another escort, and privileges would be stripped away again.

Over the next couple of weeks, I volunteered for every detail or bullshit mission that came my way. I followed every order to the T. I even tried to impress First Sergeant Fairman with my physical training (PT) skills. Any soldier who can run four miles can't be that bad of a soldier. I once again tried to humanize myself. I figured it's easy to give a criminal a hard time, but it's much harder to be vindictive to a man with hopes and fears. It's even harder to be hurtful to someone with the same common interests as yourself, maybe even someone who reminds you of yourself when you were younger. First Sergeant Fairman and I became quick friends. Being the only war vets in a group of broke dicks naturally separated us from them. We ran together, ate together, and laughed together. It was the first time in a long time that I was treated like a regular soldier.

I continued to get back into my soldier mind-set while also trying to concentrate on my legal situation. Concentrate, who am I kidding? I met with my lawyer once. He came to the conclusion that I made a bad decision that night, but I did nothing malicious. He said if I had to do time, he could probably get the sentence down to one or two years. That was unacceptable. I hadn't come this far to go back to jail, but I knew that this lawyer wasn't working for the Army, and what he said was probably right on cue. If there was a time for acceptance, that would have been it, but acceptance is for men who aren't strong enough to change things.

On one evening of the next week, First Sergeant Fairman and the commander of the broke-dicks approached me with a proposition.

Col. Goodman: mid 50's, 5'8". The colonel didn't show himself much, but then again, as the commander of a bunch of broke dicks, he didn't need to. He walked with a sense honor, some might even call it regal. He put a lot of trust in First Sergeant Fairman and didn't seem to micromanage: a quality not often found in officers.

They'd bring me out for some drinks if I told them the story that made me the dangerous, infamous man who stood before them. Curiosity killed the cat. I agreed, and we began to drink. Pitcher after pitcher, I spilled my guts. I told them the same story that I told here. I guess I'm much better of a storyteller than a story writer because they understood and sympathized with what I had done. They claimed that they might have done the same. These two men were men, not brainwashed fucks who answered harmoniously with the rest of the military.

The next morning, I received a phone call from my lawyer. It was too early, and I was still a little drunk, so I didn't take it. Then Hilderbrant stepped up to stare down at me.

"They're looking for you. I think that you have to go to court today or to see the prosecutors. I don't know."

I jumped up and threw my clothes on. Did I tell the story to two men working for the prosecutor? Did my lawyer try to call me and tell me that I was late for court? I was still too drunk to try to figure it out. I just jumped in the van and got out when they told me to. The same lady who told me that the charges were being picked up again that morning brought worse news. They were dropping all federal charges and making it a field grade. I'm sure that that sounds good to the untrained ear, but to me it sounded like they were sending me back to my old unit to be ruled over by men who were bloodthirsty for me. Of course, they couldn't sentence me for as long, but they were definitely going to give me the max, and I believe that was three years. They were finally going to win. No judges, lawyers, or weeping mothers needed, just the colonel, Chip, and me. I had no say in that room, and those two pricks were beyond content with putting me away forever. I called my lawyer back.

"Congratulations!" he said, like I had just won something.

"Fuck you, apparently I don't need you anymore. You just got me thrown in jail."

My lawyer got paid twenty thousand dollars to see me once and to pick up the phone once, and the phone call took five seconds.

I'm in the wrong business. Wondering if the bar was open yet, I stormed out the door like a pissed-off teenager. I didn't make it to the steps before First Sergeant Fairman caught up with me.

"Hey, Doc, I couldn't help but hear your phone conversation. Is everything all right?"

"No, First Sergeant, they're sending me back to my unit. I'm going to be judged there."

"Isn't that a good thing?"

"No, First Sergeant, no it's not."

"You think they're going to hang you?"

"Yeah, I'm not going to make it out of this one."

"I'm sorry to hear that. I guess I should go get your paperwork together."

I went to my room and started packing. Hilderbrant told me a story about sleeping with his half sister to cheer me up. It didn't work, and yes, I said it right, his half sister, not stepsister. Once again my head hit my hands.

The next morning at PT, I was called out of formation. I was told to get dressed and report to Col. Goodman's office at 9:00 a.m. Everything was packed, and I was ready to be escorted wherever the hell I was being escorted to. I was in front of the door at 9:00 a.m. with bells on. I knocked and went through the whole rigamarole of military etiquette. When I opened the door, Col. Goodman was sitting and First Sergeant Fairman was standing with a smile from ear to ear.

"Sir, First Sergeant, good morning."

Col. Goodman held the conversation through the entire thing. "Good morning, Doc."

He was flipping through a file on his desk before looking up at me.

"Doc, we're here to determine whether you were at fault for the charges pending against you. This is a formal field grade Article 15 hearing, and anything you have to say will be taken into consideration by the first sergeant and me. Do you understand what I've just told you?"

"No, sir. I..."

"I'll tell you what, let me finish before you go on. The federal charges against you have been dropped. Due to lack of evidence and what they think will be a waste of taxpayers' money, it has been reduced to a field grade Article 15. Now, through my experience with you I've only seen the mentality of an ideal soldier, especially under your circumstances. You've complied with everything that I've asked of you. The first sergeant agrees with me and adds that he doesn't think he's seen a better soldier come through my company, and that's my point. You were attached to *my company* by your unit, which means your company commander is me. Which means any judicial action that can be taken against you can be taken by me."

A smile crept across my face. Soon, none of us could hide our teeth. Again, I was tearing up.

"Doc, do you have anything to add before we make our decision?"

"No, sir."

"I do have one question. You were stripped of all of your rank prior to this event. Why?"

"A wine still, sir. I made and sold wine and was caught." I didn't feel I had to go into detail.

"OK. We find you innocent of all charges due to lack of evidence. Until further evidence is revealed, you are free to go. Welcome home, Doc."

"Thank you, sir."

Then the first sergeant spoke up. "This only works under one condition."

"Anything, First Sergeant."

"You think I can get a bottle of that wine?"

Obviously joking, we all began to laugh.

"C'mon, Doc, I'll escort you to the bus stop."

I stopped for a second and started to smile. "Escort me, huh? I think I can take care of it, but thank you anyway."

Afterword

In the military, as in life, there are leaders and there are followers; both are needed, but first, things must be understood about both. Leadership cannot be taught by any textbook or by any numbers of years in college; it is not a skill that you sharpen, and it is definitely not something you brag about. True leaders learn what they know through experience, most likely through their mistakes, mistakes that they take full responsibility for. These are men who do not have to demand respect, but to whom it is given freely. It is possible to get a small following with a sharp tongue, but it's the actions of the individual that makes him or her a real leader. Any man who blames his mistakes on anything other than himself is a fraud and is most likely at the top of any chain of command, whether it be military or business. Sadly, we have to deal with these people to get anywhere in life, so for that, this is my advice for the followers. Find a good leader, one who will teach you through his experiences, who will not try to embarrass you or blame you, and then learn, and one day, you may be a hell of a leader yourself. And for those who lead, you don't need my advice; just take care of your boys and don't get into the drug smuggling market; it causes more problems than you might think.

In respect for the broken families that this war has created, I have a little advice for the heavy brass. We are only human, with human emotions, human needs, and most of all we make human mistakes. A year away from everything you love can tear down even the toughest man. Six-month tours with no R&R and stay-in-place equipment passed on from unit to unit should alleviate some of the costs, financially and pertaining to the families. Six months away from your wife or husband is doable, but after a year, it's as if you have grown apart. Also, spend less money on the god damn food; half the sons of bitches who stay on base gain twenty pounds eating three times a day. PT scores are lower, females are fatter, and millions of dollars are wasted. Chicken patties, not lobster. Mystery meat, not two-inch steak. I'm sure you'll catch on one day.

As for the women, I know this book doesn't depict them as soldiers equal to their male counterparts, but you must remember that I left the war part out. So here's a little taste. While I was on gate guard, one of my female counterparts shot and killed four insurgents, wielding a rocket-propelled grenade launcher. She killed four more of the enemy than I did. Without hesitation, or a thought of equality, she did the only job that every soldier is built for. My hat's off to all the females who fought.

Index of Names

Tank	123
The Colonel	38
The Scallywags	52
Topp	30
Sgt. Buck	76
Sgt. Fish	104
Sgt. Hottie	105
Sgt. Joe	75
Sgt. Lt.	7
Sgt. Maj.	12
Sgt. Stress	104
Sgt. Waterfalls	119
Short Stuff	15
Slim w/the Tilt	45
Spc. Sexy	106
Wild Bill	6

Rank Structure and Terminology

		Enlisted
Sergeant Major	SGM	E-9
First Sergeant	1SG	E-8
Master Sergeant	MSG	E-8
Sergeant First Class	SFC	E-7
Staff Sergeant	SSG	E-6
Sergeant	SGT	E-5
Specialist	SPC	E-4
Private First Class	PFC	E-3
Private	PV2	E-2
Private	PVT	E-1

		Officers
Colonel	COL	O-6
Lieutenant Colonel	LTC	O-5
Major	MAJ	O-4
Captain	CPT	O-3
First Lieutenant	1LT	O-2
Second Lieutenant	2LT	O-1

Made in the USA
Lexington, KY
13 December 2009